# ELECTRIC VEHICLES AND THE

# JAGUAR I-PACE

## DAVID J. BRICKNELL

# Copyright

## Acknowledgements

I should like to thank the various EV groups and forums for the inspiration for this book. This book covers the subjects that are regularly raised by owners of EVs.

Cover photograph courtesy of Daniel Bohmer and Tim Sture.

## Foreword by Tom Moloughney

It's abundantly clear that we're on the precipice of seismic changes in the automotive world. Legacy automakers are struggling to move quickly enough to adapt to a market that's evolving at a rate faster than what they are accustomed to.

There's going to be casualties! This may come as a surprise to many, but I believe that not every established auto manufacturer selling vehicles today will be in business in 10 or 15 years. New comers, focusing solely on electric cars such as Tesla are taking market share at an alarming rate. There's also well-funded all-electric upstarts such as Nio and Byton from China. Both of which have their sights on global distribution within a few short years. Yes, the times they are a-changing.

I've been blogging and writing for some of the most popular electric vehicle news outlets for about ten years now, which is how long I've been driving electric. Five years ago, I started a consulting company, Charging Ahead EV Consulting, to work with the various stakeholders in the electric vehicle industry, as I could clearly see where the industry was going.

One of the first manufacturers that reached out to me for advice was Jaguar Land Rover. I have to admit, I was surprised at the time. JLR is a relatively small company, compared to automotive giants like Volkswagen, Daimler, Toyota, General Motors, etc. At the time, I didn't think the smaller OEMs would be ready to make the tremendous investment necessary to develop an electric vehicle program. I was wrong.

After spending some time in 2014 with the small iMobility team that JLR had assembled, I was convinced that they were just as certain that the future of the auto industry was electric as I was. Back then the Jaguar I-Pace was nothing more than an idea on paper, but the JLR team was laser-focused on making the first all-electric Jaguar a winner. The fact that they were reaching out to people like me who weren't industry insiders, but instead people living with electric cars, so that they could better understand what customers want in an EV really impressed me.

I was introduced to David Bricknell online, in electric vehicle groups on Facebook. I started the BMW i3 Facebook group and David was a member. One of the best things about Facebook groups is the amazing amount of information from crowdsourcing that the group provides. When one member asks a question about the car, there are dozens of members who offer a reply within minutes. This is extremely helpful to new or perspective buyers, especially because electric cars are different than any other car they've owned before. Questions about batteries, charging, regenerative braking and even electric wiring are asked on a daily basis.

While many members contribute, there's a small group of people who have a better understanding of some of the more technical issues, and are able to add valuable insight to the discussions. David is one of those talented people. I suppose it's partly due to his engineering background, and partly because of his passion for electric mobility, but David's insights have helped many people better understand the electric cars that they were driving.

But contributing in online forums and Face book Groups wasn't satisfying enough for David. In 2016 he published a book entitled "Electric Vehicles and the BMW i3". There, David put together information he collected over the past few years, along with graphs and charts on charging, range and more. It is an extremely thorough book, and one that I recommend to anyone who owns or is interested in the BMW i3. David then published his second book, which covers many of the popular EVs in production called "Joining the Electric Vehicle Revolution: The things you need to know about how your EV works.

These two books are very informative, and have been extremely helpful. Electric vehicles are different from internal combustion vehicles in many ways. While EVs are simpler, they require the owner to think differently than they always have, particularly about refueling, and that's a difficult ask. We've all become very comfortable with how we refuel an internal combustion vehicle. We may not like going to a petrol station and refueling, but since the industry has had 100 years to refine the process, it's become accessible, safe and easy.

That's not the case with electric vehicle refueling. EV charging is just beginning to proliferate, and most new owners really don't understand much more than they plug in, and at some point, the car is recharged. David explains the charging process, and provides graphs that demonstrate the charging profiles, along with taper rates of different EVs. One of the big impediments to accelerating EV adoption is getting people to understand them better, and David's books really help in that regard.

Fast forward to 2018, four years after I spent time with JLR's iMobility team, and Jaguar began to sell the car we were working on. It is their first all-electric vehicle, the I-Pace. In doing so, JLR beat Mercedes, BMW, Audi and all of the other luxury brands to market with a long-range, luxury electric car that can compete head-to-head with Tesla. Until now, Tesla has owned the entire market of premium, long-range electric vehicles; there was literally no competition. However, that's changing. Not only has Jaguar brought a competitive, desirable EV to market, but soon so will Audi, then Mercedes and then BMW. Competition is good, and I believe it will only make Tesla and the other OEMs work even harder for that competitive advantage.

So, it's probably no surprise to learn that I was thrilled to hear David was turning his attention to the I-Pace, and was writing this book. As an electric vehicle advocate, I welcome and applaud David's efforts to help people better understand electric vehicles. As someone who really likes the I-Pace, and was also consulted upon by JLR during its formative years, I look forward to reading his latest work. I hope this book helps many to better understand the I-Pace, and I also hope David continues to advocate and educate. Keep Calm and Charge On!

## Preface

In 2016, after buying my first Electric Vehicle and realising that there were many things to know about how they worked, I wrote my first book on EVs specifically addressing the BMW i3, following this with a book covering nine other EVs. This book returns to the single model format and covers the exciting new Jaguar I-Pace.

I hope this book will provide the insights into the technologies and performances of the Jaguar's first Electric Vehicle.

February 2019

David J. Bricknell CEng FRINA BSc(Hons)

This page intentionally blank

## Abbreviations

| | |
|---|---|
| AC | Alternating Current |
| A/C | Air Conditioning |
| APRF | Advanced Powertrain Research Facility - Argonne Laboratories |
| Ah | Amp Hours |
| apu | Auxiliary Power Unit |
| AVT-INL | Advanced Vehicle Testing - Idaho National laboratory |
| BEV | Battery Electric Vehicle |
| BEVx | BEV Extender |
| BMS | Battery Management System |
| CARB | California Air Resources Board |
| C-rate | Charge/discharge rate |
| CC | Constant Current |
| CCS | Combined Charging System |
| CdA | Drag Coefficient x Frontal Area |
| $CO_2$ | Carbon Dioxide |
| CSSU | Cell Supervision Sensor Unit |
| CV | Constant Voltage |
| DC | Direct Current |
| DOD | Depth of Discharge |
| DSC | Dynamic Stability Control |
| EDME | Electrical Digital Machine Electronics |
| EME | Electrical Machine Electronics |
| EPA | Environmental Protection Agency |
| EV | Electric Vehicle |
| GWP | Global Warming Potential |
| HV | High Voltage |
| HFC | HydroFlouroCarbons |
| HSM | Hybrid Synchronous Machine |
| ICE | Internal Combustion Engine |
| IEC | International Electrotechnical Commission |
| IGBT | Insulated-Gate Bipolar Transistors |

| | |
|---|---|
| IM | Induction Motor |
| kW | kiloWatt |
| kWh | kiloWatt hour |
| LCO | Lithium Cobalt Oxide |
| LFP | Lithium Iron (Ferrous) Phosphate |
| LIB | Lithium Ion Battery |
| LMO | Lithium Manganese Oxide |
| LNO | Lithium Nickel Oxide |
| LRU | Lowest Replaceable Unit |
| LTO | Lithium Titanate Oxide |
| LV | Low Voltage |
| MCR | Maximum Continuous Rating |
| N&V | Noise and Vibration |
| NCA | Nickel Cobalt Aluminium |
| NEDC | New European Driving Cycle |
| Nm | Newton metre |
| NMC | Nickel Manganese Cobalt |
| NMH | Nickel-Metal Hydride |
| PMSM | Permanent Magnet Synchronous Machine |
| PMSRM | Permanent Magnet Synchronous Reluctance Machine |
| rpm | revolution per minute |
| RFID | Radio Frequency IDentification |
| SOC | State of Charge |
| SOH | State of Health |
| THD | Total Harmonic Distortion |
| WLTP | Worldwide harmonised Light vehicle Test Procedure |
| ZEV | Zero Emissions Vehicle |

# Table of Contents

David J Bricknell

This page intentionally blank

# Introduction

This book looks at the key technologies and performances that apply to the Jaguar I-Pace and other Electric Vehicles.

The I-Pace is a 'clean-sheet' EV design adopting components from other Jaguars only where this doesn't compromise the result. The design looks a little like an SUV but it is maybe more a cab-forward fast hatchback with a very spacious interior although it does have good off-road capability.

*Distinctively shaped cab-forward Jaguar I-Pace.*
*(Photo Alexander Migl CCA by SA4.0)*

| Jaguar I-Pace | | |
|---|---|---|
| Max Speed | mph | 124 |
| | kph | 200 |
| 0-62mph/100kph | | 4.8 |
| Kerb Weight eu | kg | 2133 |
| | lb | 4702 |
| Cd | | 0.29 |
| Motor Power (max) Front | kW | 147 |
| | hp | 197 |
| Motor Power (max) Rear | kW | 147 |
| | hp | 197 |

| Range | | | |
|---|---|---|---|
| EPA Combined | Miles | 234 | |
| | km | 377 | |
| WLTP | | Lower | Higher |
| | Miles | 260 | 298 |
| | km | 418 | 480 |
| | mi/kWh | 2.6 | 2.9 |
| | km/kWh | 4.2 | 4.7 |

For those that have driven a combustion-engined Jaguar, it becomes immediately obvious that the **dynamics** of the I-Pace are different: the instant torque giving smooth and immediately available acceleration and energy regeneration providing simple one-pedal driving.

The **battery** is of course the key to mobile electric transportation and today's battery developments are core to the recent rapid uptake of EVs. The historical battery types and the technological reasons for the current dominance of the Lithium Ion Battery LIB are discussed together with the various electrode chemistries and competing cell formats. Battery performance and life, a whole new area for most EV drivers, are discussed and near/medium term future developments are also addressed.

A battery is an accumulator and stores energy generated elsewhere. Once depleted, **recharging** is necessary. For the most part EVs are recharged at home, often whilst the owner is sleeping. On-route charging infrastructure is still growing rapidly both in number and in charging power but for the moment, is a labyrinth of different charging cards and payment types. Thankfully, agreed plug standards are now being implemented throughout most of the world's different regions.

Energy stored in the battery is delivered through **power electronics to the motors**. Power Electronics have been key to maximizing energy efficiency through efficient control of the motor. Manufacturers are currently adopting different motor technologies to address different pressures of costs, size, efficiency and environmental friendliness; some manufacturers are buying in this technology and some are investing in their own developments and Intellectual Property IP.

It often comes as a surprise to EV drivers that their electric car has a radiator. **Cooling of key drivetrain components,** particularly battery, motor and power-electronics, is the key to sustaining high performance.

Whilst cabin cooling through air-conditioning is much the same as combustion engine cars, **heating** is quite different as there is no 'free' waste heat from the combustion engine. For EVs with relatively small battery packs, heating can be a significant drain in deepest winter but as battery capacity increases this becomes less of an issue.

The **environment** and the increasingly tighter **regulations** surrounding transport is one of the reasons for the latest growth of EVs. Both Green House Gases GHGs and 'toxic pollution' are addressed and are often in opposition – one of the key mistakes behind the push for increased diesel adoption was the rush for lower $CO_2$ at the expense of increased NOx and PMs. Both of these emissions are addressed.

Wherever possible the charts included in this book are multi-axes in order to avoid repetitively showing the same information each using System International SI, Imperial, and the UK's hybrid of SI-Imperial. Whilst the charts are a little busier to read, this is considered preferable to including three versions of each chart.

# Dynamics and Performance

## Overview

The I-Pace was eagerly awaited as being the first serious Tesla competitor from a major, performance-oriented, traditional car manufacturer. Reception has been enthusiastic with construction and assembly standards being very high and acceleration and handling matching well with the Jaguar purist's expectations.

The power and the energy required to drive a vehicle are the same whether it comes from a tank of fossil fuel and a combustion engine or from a battery and electric motor – the differences are in the technology that translates the energy into power.

Electric motors make EVs both easy and fun to drive; they have rapid and responsive acceleration, one-pedal driving, no clutch and only one fixed gear.

Keeping the battery discharge rate, the rate at which you extract energy from the battery, low enough to prolong battery life is important as is keeping the motor and motor drive (inverter) within their temperature limits. Both of these issues are key to higher performance and to higher continuous speeds.

Range is a product of the battery capacity energy against the energy used for accelerating and for sustaining speed. Battery capacity though isn't an absolute value - it varies with cell temperature, with rate of charge and discharge, with calendar time and with the number of charge/discharge cycles. Range also varies with vehicle speed in exactly the same way as it does in a combustion engine vehicle – the faster you go the quicker the energy store is depleted whether this is a battery or a fuel tank.

Cabin cooling is well understood with Internal Combustion Engine or ICE cars but for an EV the amount of energy required for cabin heating in colder climes comes as a considerable surprise to most. As with many EV manufacturers, the I-Pace comes with an Eco-Mode that reduces non-essential energy users thereby maximizing range.

Cabin heating of an ICE car is essentially done using (free) waste heat whereas the I-Pace, along with other EVs, has to generate it from the same battery energy that also provides range. Jaguar has adopted a heat pump and coupled it with power electronics and motor waste heat to maximize efficiency.

EVs are zero-emissions at the point of use - emissions are not often considered to be a performance-criteria but for today's combustion engines it is the technical area that is demanding most investment. EV emissions are related to the electrical energy generation source: in most countries power station emissions are lower per kWh than those produced by ICE vehicles.

## Key Components

Electric Vehicles all use essentially the same key components albeit they use different variants of each component type. Jaguar has developed much of these technologies and equipment themselves including the motors and the battery pack, although not the cells.

Equipment includes:

A **High-Voltage HV battery pack** - in automotive terms, high-voltage means typically 300V-450V although 800V and above can be expected in the future. HV batteries are today always variants of Lithium Ion using different configurations (cylinder/prismatic or pouch), different chemistries (NCA, LMO, NMC electrodes and liquid or polymer electrolytes), and different configurations (serial or serial/parallel, depending on the cell capacity and power required). The I-Pace uses 432 NMC pouch cells at a system 450V. Jaguar do not state who the cell supplier is but it is widely believed to be LG Chem.

A **Low Voltage LV battery**, usually 12V, is used for initialising the HV system, for powering the systems used for accessing the car, and for systems such as the alarm system and entertainment.

A **motor or motors** usually either an Asynchronous (Induction Machine) or a Synchronous Machine. Motors can be arranged to drive the front wheels, the rear wheels, both front and rear wheels and even all four independently. Permanent magnet synchronous motors use either ferrous or rare-earth permanent magnets whilst Wound Synchronous does not. Induction Motors also do not use Rare Earth Magnets. Highly controllable power electronics has enabled reluctance motors to be used providing the highest levels of efficiency. Jaguar has developed its own Spoke-Type Interior Permanent Magnet Motor driving through an epicyclic gear through the centre of the motor – this makes it very compact and enables motors to be fitted front and back with minimal cabin intrusion.

Road capable EVs all use a **single-speed fixed gear** - motors have sufficient torque and rpm range to enable the use of a single-speed gearbox giving a credible top-speed with good acceleration and uninterrupted energy regeneration. Full torque at zero-speed eliminates the need for a clutch.

A **drive or inverter/rectifier** is used to convert battery DC to 3-phase AC (and back again during regeneration), and for controlling vehicle speed. Today's Inverters all utilise power electronics/IGBTs, either in a six-pack or multiple six-packs depending upon the total power required: each pair addressing one of the phases and each one within the pair addressing the positive or negative part of the AC wave. Each motor will have its own dedicated inverter drive.

A **cooling system** is necessary for the electronic and electrical components, usually involving a water-glycol mix circulating through the components and then shedding heat through a front mounted radiator/fan combination.

A **battery cooling system** for use during hard driving, long journeys or when charging at elevated temperatures. This system can be forced air, water-glycol or a refrigerant system. Few EV manufacturers retain passive thermal management. Jaguar uses a combination of water-glycol and refrigeration in order to optimize efficiency.

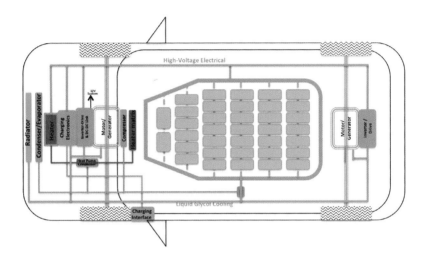

*Key-Components schematic showing the HV electrical components and the cooling systems.*

## Overall Vehicle Efficiency

As with any propulsion system, losses are incurred at every energy conversion. Battery Electric Vehicles are very efficient at converting grid-derived electricity into vehicle motion. There are inefficiencies or losses in the national distribution grid, the charging rectifier, the round trip to and from the battery, the motor drive inverter, the motor, and the gear and final drive.

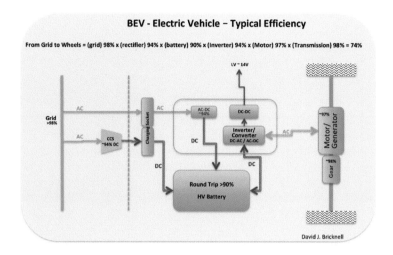

*Typical efficiency of a Battery Electric Vehicle*

## Resistance and Power

At a steady speed (on level ground and with no wind) there are two principal components of a vehicle's resistance: rolling resistance and aerodynamic resistance   - accelerating the vehicle will also require energy to overcome kinetic resistance. Wind and hills will also affect vehicle resistance either up or down.  Vehicle weight is the key factor for rolling resistance whereas the vehicle's frontal area and its drag coefficient are the key factors for aerodynamic resistance.  Aerodynamic resistance dominates at higher vehicle speeds whereas rolling resistance dominates at lower speeds.

**Rolling Resistance** accounts for the energy required to overcome the resistance offered by the tyre during rotation.  All Vehicles, EVs as well as ICE, drive through wheels and pneumatic tyres.

As a good approximation the force required to overcome rolling resistance is proportional to the weight of the vehicle and the coefficient of rolling resistance; the greater the vehicle weight and the higher the tyre's rolling coefficient the higher the resistance and the more power that is required.  For a vehicle's pneumatic tyre, the coefficient of rolling resistance will increase a little as vehicle speed increases but this increase is small in comparison to the increases in aerodynamic resistance at higher speeds.   Resistance will increase when going uphill in response to the car's weight and relative to the steepness of the hill, and equally it will decrease when going downhill.

**Aerodynamic Resistance** accounts for the energy required to propel the vehicle through the air.  Resistance is proportional to the square of the vehicle speed and power is proportional to the cube of the speed.

Air density changes will have an effect on resistance offering higher aerodynamic resistance at colder temperatures due to denser air.

Wind speed will either increase aerodynamic resistance (head winds) or decrease aerodynamic resistance (tail winds) thereby either increasing or decreasing the power required to maintain a speed.

Reducing the frontal area of the vehicle to improve the aerodynamics will normally lead to an increase in vehicle length if internal volume is to be maintained and increasing vehicle length will increase weight and so a balance has to be sought between lowering rolling resistance and lowering aerodynamic drag.

The cross-over point between rolling resistance and aerodynamic resistance will vary between vehicles depending on the relative balance between weight and aerodynamics.

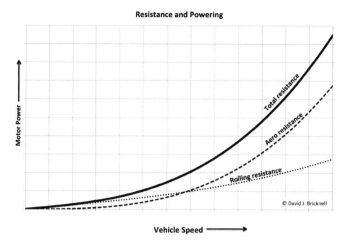

*The illustration above is for a generic vehicle, ICE and EV, showing the contributions from both rolling and aerodynamic drag:*

*Total Resistance is the sum of Rolling Resistance, Aerodynamic Resistance and Drive Train inefficiencies.*

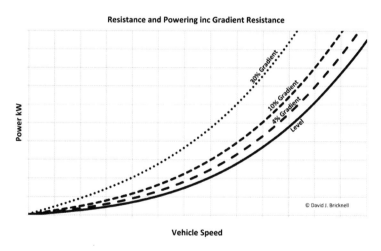

*Hills have a significant impact on vehicle power requirements – the above chart shows the increase from typical motorway/highways, major trunk roads and other roads.*

**Power** (kW or hp) is a measure of force multiplied by speed – for an ICE or an electric motor this is torque multiplied by rpm.

The power curve for an ICE and an electric motor are quite different: an electric motor can deliver maximum torque at zero rpm and it's this characteristic that allows an EV to do without a clutch, and to manage with a single stage fixed gear whilst still delivering high power and rapid, smooth acceleration at low speeds. An ICE on the other hand requires a clutch to ensure the engine doesn't stall as power is delivered to the wheels and requires multiple gears to ensure performance through the vehicle's speed range.

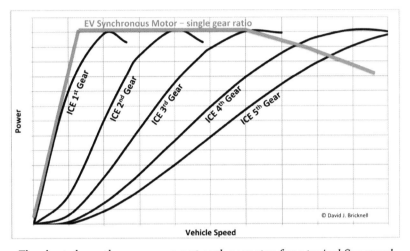

*The chart shows the power curve at each gear step for a typical five speed ICE vehicle contrasted with a single-speed electric motor EV.*

# Range

The range of a vehicle will depend upon how quickly it uses its stored energy: energy is used to overcome resistance (rolling and aero), to overcome inefficiencies in the drivetrain (gears, bearings, etc.), to power the cars electronics, entertainment systems, lights, wipers, etc. (a rather small amount), to cool the cabin, and to heat the cabin (more significant for an EV than an ICE).

Range can be further improved by selecting ECO driving mode instead of comfort. The Eco mode turns off heated seats, climate seats, heated wheel, heated windshield and reduces blower or fan speed.

Early EVs were generally heavier than a similar ICE but improved battery energy density and bespoke electric vehicle designs have now narrowed the gap.

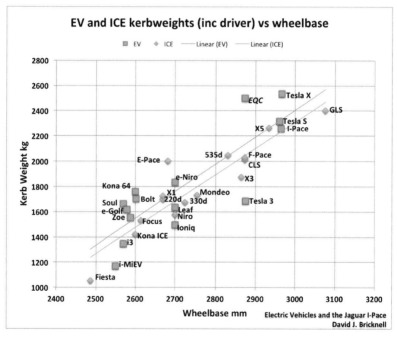

*Chart showing Kerb Weight against Wheelbase for both EV and ICE. The difference in weight has narrowed significantly and, in some case, swung in favour of EVs.*

**For an ICE vehicle**, transmission inefficiency at lower speeds can be significant (modern ICE usually have more than five gears with some having up to nine) as is combustion inefficiency (for a petrol/gasoline car around 25% efficiency, reducing as rpm decreases). Cooling using air conditioning does reduce range, but heating of the cabin is done with waste combustion heat and hence doesn't impact range.

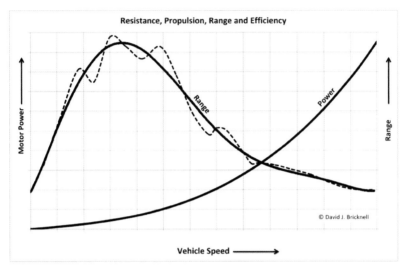

*A range chart for a typical ICE powered vehicle would include the efficiency of the engine and transmission during each of the gear changes. Compared to an EV the efficiency at lower speeds is much reduced.*

**For an EV** the energy stored in the battery is used for motion, overcoming transmission inefficiency and electronics losses, and for cooling, and, because there is little waste heat from inefficiencies, also for heating the cabin. However, transmission inefficiency is considerably less as EVs either use a single locked-train gear or, in the case of the I-Pace, a single stage epicyclic gear integrated with the differential. Motor efficiencies are also high and motor efficiency at lower speeds remain high when adopting permanent magnet motors that eliminate the energising losses of an induction motor. In a number of new EVs, two (or three) motors are used to further reduce drivetrain inefficiencies at lower speeds (and to maximize energy regeneration) better matching power available to that demanded.

On a level road, the range curve for an EV shows a peak at very low speeds decreasing as rolling resistance increases and reducing more rapidly as aerodynamic losses build up. Increasing aerodynamic resistance is the most significant contributor to reduced range at higher speeds for both ICE and EV although there is a small contribution from loss of effective battery capacity from a higher energy discharge rate (C-rate) at higher vehicle speeds. The peak occurs due to low speed motor inefficiencies albeit these can be quite small.

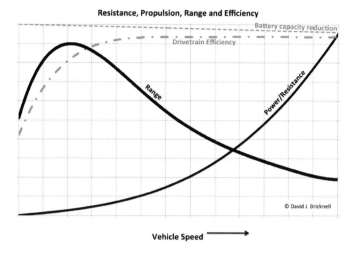

Resistance, Propulsion, Range and Efficiency

Vehicle Speed

Official range figures the I-Pace are:

- WLTP range
  - 298miles / 480km (most efficient version)
  - 260 miles / 418km (least efficient version)
- EPA (combined) Range 234miles / 377km.

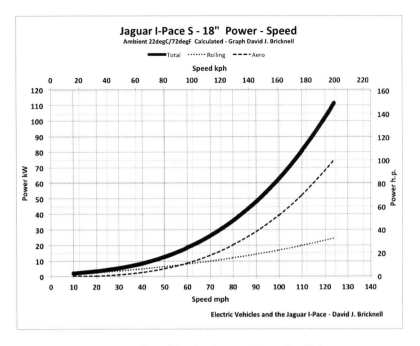

*Power - Speed for the Jaguar I-Pace S – 18"*

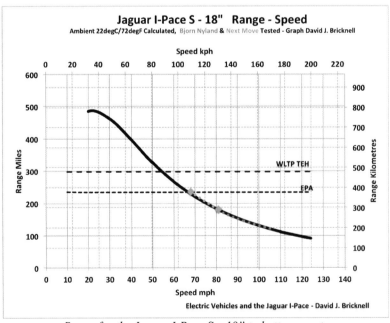

*Range for the Jaguar I-Pace S – 18" to battery empty*

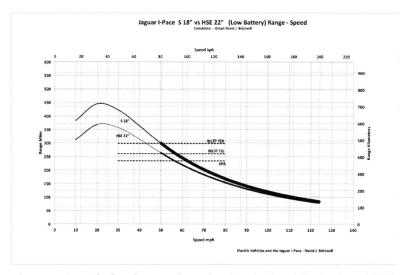

*Comparative calculated range chart showing the S on 18" wheels and HSE on 22" wheels: the range shown is to 'low battery warning' which is about 10-15 miles remaining.*

Losses due to cooling the cabin with air conditioning reduce range in both EVs and in ICE. Cabin heating however is the area of significant difference to ICE vehicles. In order to heat the cabin EVs use battery energy to heat the cabin either through resistive heating (as in an electric kettle), which can be quite energy intensive, or heat pump (reverse of a refrigeration system) but in both cases battery energy is used and hence range is reduced and, because heating is time related and propulsion is speed related, the peak range point increases as ambient temperature reduces or cabin heating load increases. Heating for an ICE makes use of waste heat from inefficient combustion and hence does not impact on range.

The I-Pace introduces a further improvement in efficiency by utilizing waste heat from cooling of electrical and electronics including using this to improve heat pump efficiency.

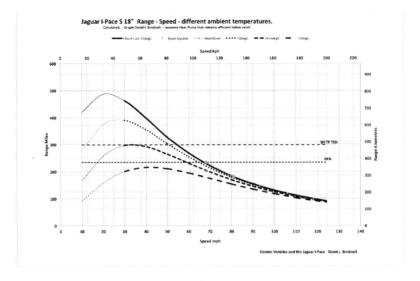

*Charts showing the range impact of ambient temperature variation through the I-Pace's speed range. Above is the S with 18" wheels, below the HSE with 22"/*

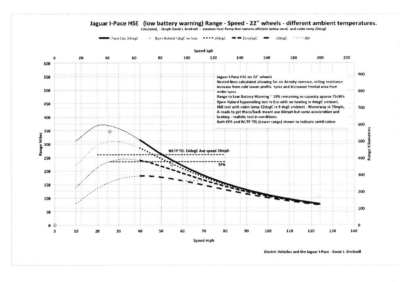

*Temperature has less impact at higher speeds as heating is time related and whereas propulsion is speed related – at higher speeds there isn't enough time to use the heating load.*

18

Range is also affected by driving style and route and road type: average speeds are higher on highways and motorways and slower with more acceleration and braking when driving in cities. Aggressive or enthusiastic driving will also affect range. Both ICE and EVs are affected similarly if there is reduced opportunity to regenerate energy.

The chart below shows the range variation from different driving cycles representing city and highway/motorway as well as an aggressive style and these are plotted against external ambient temperature with a comfortable target cabin temperature

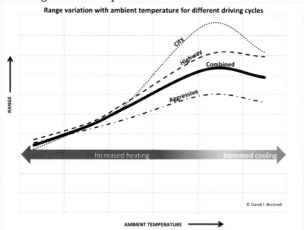

The graph combines the contribution of three things to the reduction in range due to ambient temperature change.

The battery capacity is reduced as Li-Ion batteries are less willing to give up charge when cold but this is quite small compared to the heating energy usage.

There is an increase in vehicle drag due to increased air density although this is quite small compared to the other factors.

The largest change comes from the heating or cooling load. EVs have little or no waste heat with which to heat the cabin and have to generate it from resistive heating coil. A heat pump can help to reduce heating load although as the temperature drops the efficiency of the heat pump reduces as the difference in temperature of the ambient air with the refrigerant reduces. Some EVs now use the waste heat from the motor and inverter cooling to improve heat pump performance at very low ambient temperatures.

Preconditioning an EV whilst plugged-in will help range mostly by warming or cooling the cabin and by warming the battery: preheating the battery does make a small difference in battery capacity but a quite significant range improvement because energy can be regenerated into a warmer battery from the beginning of the journey.

Given the impact of heating on an EV's range there is quite evidently a difference in achievable range throughout the year- the extent of which depends upon variation in ambient temperatures throughout the year.

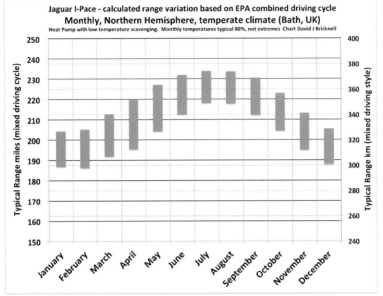

*Variation in range throughout the year*
*(Northern Hemisphere – Bath, UK and Montreal, Canada).*

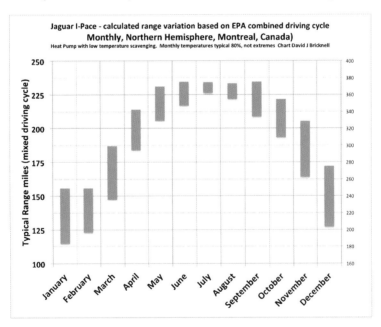

## Acceleration and maximum continuous speed

Those new to EVs are always surprised to find how easy they are to drive quickly: instant torque, no gear changes and high excess-power all contribute to a very spirited drive. Equally, it can be a surprise to find that maximum speed can be rather more restricted than in a comparable ICE although always in excess of most maximum speed limits with a few exceptions only. Recent EVs with large battery capacities are now achieving electronically-limited maximum speeds similar to comparable ICE.

Three things will normally contribute to the EVs maximum speed: Motor continuous power (can be around half of the rated maximum power); Inverter continuous power (again can be considerably less than the rated maximum power); and battery discharge rate (typically 1-C for continuous, 2-C limited time, and maybe up to 8-C for acceleration power).

These limitations are shown on the chart below

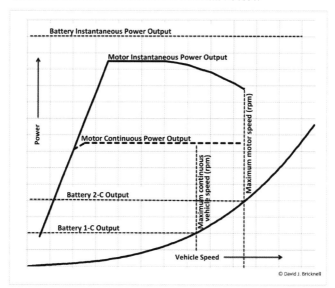

Cooling of these components is essential for sustaining high power / high speeds or for aggressive driving involving high acceleration and sharp braking. The Battery Management System BMS will reduce power available from the battery if sustained high discharge rates are likely to impact on battery life. Probably inverter cooling will be critical before motor maximum temperatures are reached but both components will cause a reduction in available power if a lot of acceleration and braking causes high component temperatures.

## Driving Styles and Regeneration

How an EV is driven has a considerable impact on battery capacity and vehicle range as well as on battery life.  One area where EVs differ from ICE cars is in their ability to regenerate driving energy back into the battery: in city driving cycles in warmer weather this can recover up to 40% energy although when on a motorway or highway the opportunity for regeneration is typically less than 10% energy. When the battery is very cold, regeneration is restricted or prevented by the battery management system to avoid cell damage.

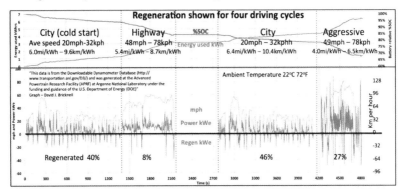

*This chart (based on a BMW i3 but the principle is the same across all EVs) shows the impact of different driving cycles on the rate of energy usage for an EV.  Cold and hot start city driving is shown as well as highway and aggressive driving.  Regeneration during each of the four different driving cycles can be seen – during highway driving regen contributes little but during city driving it can be a quite significant range-improving energy-saving measure.*

For the i-Pace, regeneration occurs as you lift off the accelerator/gas pedal and continues as the brake pedal is applied.  When braking pressure increases the friction brakes are then applied.  The level of regen is can be adjusted by the driver to either low or high.  The high level will reduce the amount of pedal changing from accelerator to brake.

The second chart in this section charts a cold-start city cycle against a hot start and the additional energy used on a cold start can be clearly seen. Some of this comes from additional heating load and that can be seen in the small disparity between the hot (in red) and cold (in blue) power and some from the fact that EVs, including the I-Pace, won't regenerate power back into the battery either at high battery SOC or at low battery temperatures - tests at -17°C/1F show the battery didn't receive any regenerated energy until some 20 minutes of city driving losing some 10% of potential recoverable energy in this test at this very low temperature.

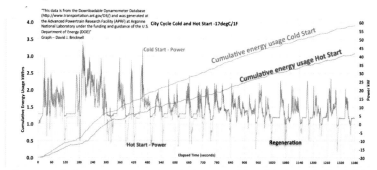

*Regenerated energy comparison between cold and hot start city driving cycles – the battery management system BMS prevents regenerating until the battery cells have warmed from driving.*

## Emissions

One of the many reasons for driving an EV is to reduce the impact on the environment and on life, particularly in towns and cities.

In assessing the impact of transport and energy generation on the environment and on the population there is often confusion between Green House Gases GHGs and Toxic Emissions.

Green House Gases GHGs include, in order of Global Warming Potential (GWP): ChloroFluoroCarbons (CFCs), Nitrous Oxide ($N_2O$, not $NO_x$), Methane $CH_4$ and Carbon Dioxide $CO_2$. CFCs were used mostly as refrigerants and are now being controlled following the Montreal Protocol (1989); they are not abundant but their GWP is some 10,000 or more times that of $CO_2$. Global Warming occurs from the Green House effect where Global Warming Gases trap heat in the atmosphere - there has been a significant increase in $CO_2$ in the atmosphere since the Industrial Revolution.

Nitrous Oxide $N_2O$ (or laughing gas) mostly comes from agriculture (about 75% from both nitrogen fixing in the soil and animal waste) but some (about 10%) also comes from vehicle emissions (ref US Energy Information Administration); it is colourless, non-toxic, and non-flammable, but has a GWP of some 300 times that of $CO_2$.

Methane is produced naturally in wetlands, is manmade by energy (gas and coal extraction), and also comes from ruminants (cows and sheep) and decaying matter. It has a GWP of some 20-70 times that of $CO_2$ but is not as abundant.

Carbon Dioxide $CO_2$ is some 200 times more abundant than Methane, which is why it makes a larger contribution to Global Warming even though its GWP is lower. $CO_2$ is not defined as a toxic gas (although some occupations (brewers and miners) are at risk from high concentrations of $CO_2$) dangerous concentrations are considered to be some 150 times atmospheric levels. $CO_2$ occurs naturally but combustion of fossil fuels for electricity, transportation and in industry is increasing the amount of $CO_2$ in the atmosphere at a rate that is accelerating Global Warming.

Toxicity, on the other hand, is dose (or concentration) dependent: the impact of the toxic emission is not detectable below a certain level and then once above that level toxicity increases as concentration increases. For vehicles, the key toxic emission of most concern is Nitrogen Dioxide (NOx). High NOx levels are related to a significant number of early deaths. Internal Combustion Engines also emit Particulates PMs (or soot), measured as $PM_{10}$ and $PM_{2.5}$ depending on the size of the particulate. These particulates are small enough to penetrate deep into the lungs. PMs are harmful at any concentration.

Diesels are two to five times worse on NOx that petrol/gasoline engines - this is a function of higher combustion temperatures and pressures. Increasing efficiency by increasing the combustion temperatures of the engine reduces $CO_2$ but increases NOx. Further increasing efficiency of the engine by lean-burn (using less fuel) renders the previously used three-way catalytic converter non functional but does then require a lean NOx trap. As well as the lean NOx trap, other methods for reducing NOx emissions include Exhaust Gas Recirculation EGR (which reduces combustion temperature but in doing so increases particulates) or Selective Catalytic Reduction SCR (using injected Urea or AdBlue into the exhaust catalyst) but this drops the engine efficiency thereby increasing $CO_2$. Some engines are adopting a Miller Cycle to further reduce NOx but without increasing PMs or lowering efficiency; the Miller cycle reduces combustion temperature by closing the intake valve early and expanding the compressed gas hence cooling it (Charles Law) but in order to regain power and efficiency requires expensive two-stage turbocharging to increase charge density.

Petrol/gasoline engines use the Otto Cycle and are lower in NOx (because combustion temperatures are lower) but higher in $CO_2$ (because efficiency is lower) but they produce very little PMs (unless they use Gas Direct Injection GDI).

Diesels produce PMs or Particulate Matter - both $PM_{10}$ and $PM_{2.5}$ are produced. There is no real threshold level for PMs; they are always very hazardous to health. PMs used to be just a diesel problem but in order to reduce $CO_2$ and improve engine efficiency, petrol/gasoline engines are now adopting Gas Direct Injection GDI that has increased particulate emissions.

For all Power Stations, including Coal, NOx levels are lower per kWh than Internal Combustion Engines and gas is a third of the NOx produced by coal. Coal and oil fired power stations will produce Sulphur Dioxides SOx as well as toxic heavy metals (mercury, lead, cadmium, etc.) which burning gas doesn't. Gas has typically 10,000 times less the amount of PMs than coal. Power Stations are generally away from town centres whereas vehicle emissions are at their most concentrated, and hence most toxic, in town centres. Emissions at the point of use are an important factor for the concentration of toxic emissions but not for $CO_2$.

In summary, containing $CO_2$ (a GHG) is important to the future of the planet and, through taxation, lower $CO_2$ emissions have affected vehicle purchases of late but $CO_2$ isn't toxic. An EV $CO_2$ footprint will be lower than for an ICE and, on a like for like vehicle basis, the $CO_2$ associated with new vehicle manufacture will quickly be paid back in a couple of years or so.

This page intentionally blank

# Battery

## Overview

The 90kWh battery pack is Jaguar's own utilizing LG-Chem's nickel rich $NMC_{622}$ pouch cells manufactured at the LG Chem factory in Wroclaw, Poland. Jaguar has included 432 cells (wide letter-box shape) in 36 modules, 12 cells per module; each cell is 58Ah at a nominal 3.6V.

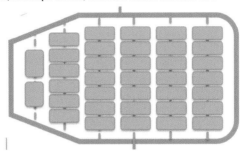

*The I-Pace battery pack has 36 modules each containing 12 pouch-type battery cells.*

The pack is configured as a 4p, 108s meaning that, unlike most other EV manufacturers using 96 cells in series, the I-Pace has a nominal pack Voltage of 388V and a maximum of 450V. This allows Jaguar to maximize the pack capacity whilst still utilising widely available electrical components.

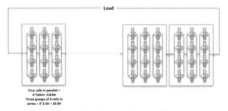

36 modules including 12 Cells. 4 in parallel and three groups of 4 cells in series

36 modules * 232Ah * 10.8V = 90.2kWh

108 groups of four cells in series - 108* 3.6V = 388V nominal

The battery pack nominal gross capacity is therefore 4 x 108 x 58Ah x 3.6V = 90.2kWh with Jaguar stating that the usable capacity is around 84.7kWh – a usable to gross of 94% which is quite high. The battery pack is capable of delivering 1000A (~400kW) and regenerate 450A (~175kW)

Jaguar's EPA submission shows a system Ah of 222.9Ah and a system nominal voltage of 388V (which, given the 4p, 108s configuration means each cell is 55.7Ah at 3.6V) giving a pack of 86.5kWh. Various consumer tests have indicated a usable capacity nearer 82kWh full to empty battery, 75kWh full to low battery warning or 66kWh 90% to low battery warning.

Jaguar manages the amount of usable capacity (depth-of-discharge) based upon both environmental (temperature) and driver (speed/acceleration/braking) inputs in order to maintain battery cell State of Health and lifetime (maintain at least 70% capacity over 8-years and 100,000miles/160,000km).

Jaguar also encourage not regularly charging to more than 90% and not frequently going below 20% - this in order to maximise cell cyclic life. – it would be expected that this would be used for most daily trips but not for longer journeys where maximizing range would be more important.

*The I-Pace battery with the cut-away showing the cells packaged within the modules. (Photo Halit Murat Gültekin)*

The battery pack is cooled by a water-glycol system that itself is cooled by the air conditioning refrigerant. Cooling is from the bottom of the pack. At lower temperatures the coolant is heated in order to try and keep cell temperature between 20 and 30°C (68 and 86 F) rather than above 10°C in order to allow regeneration of braking energy. Jaguar's Wolfgang Ziebert also states that they intend to keep the battery cell temperature within a range of +/- 2 °C to 3°C which seems rather a lot tighter a tolerance than other EV manufacturers. Whilst this will extend battery cell life it could also provide quite an increase on battery heating/cooling load.

The Lithium-Ion Battery (LIB) has probably been the single most influential development in the reintroduction of credible electric vehicles capable of challenging the dominance of ICE powered vehicles. In the last five to ten years energy density, specific energy, and cycle life have come together with significant cost reductions to make LIBs the energy storage of choice for EVs.

Most consumer electronics use LIBs with a cathode of Lithium Cobalt Oxide (LCO), and, whereas some EVs adopted Lithium Manganese Oxide (LMO) most chose Lithium Nickel Oxides, such as: Nickel Cobalt Aluminium (NCA), and Nickel Manganese Cobalt (NMC or sometimes written as NCM).

Heavier duty applications such as buses and trucks and marine vessels are also using Lithium Iron Phosphate (LFP) for long life or Lithium Titanate Oxide (LTO) where very rapid and frequent recharging is required however cost reductions of automotive NMC cells means marine is now also increasingly adopting NMC.

LIB cells are available in different formats with cylindrical, prismatic and pouch formats being used by different manufacturers. Battery packs are put together in strings of cells in series to get higher voltage and, where necessary, several parallel strings of series cells in order to get capacity.

Battery capacity isn't such an absolute value in the way that we perceive a tank of fossil fuel to be; the available capacity will depends upon the cell temperature and the rate of discharge amongst other things.

Batteries lose capacity through life, partly due to calendar ageing and partly due to charge/discharge cycling. The Battery Management System will seek to minimize damage the cycle life by restricting performance in lower or very high temperatures including reducing charging rate where necessary. Precondition of the battery in very cold weather is a user strategy for improving cell life. Cell balancing is essential to maintaining battery pack capacity.

For the future, improvements in anode and cathode materials are expected to lead to increased energy storage, improved rates of charging and increased cycle life. Considerable efforts are being made to introduce a solid electrolyte that would improve passive safety of the cell, improve cycle life and decrease charging time. EVs with large battery packs (>60kWhrs) largely solve the problems of cycle life simply by needing less charging cycles for the same number of miles or kilometers per vehicle life – EV battery life is now likely to be in the hundreds of thousands of miles or km.

## Battery Types

Battery technology has been one of the key improvements for adoption of Electric Vehicles. With little competition from the early 'explosion engines', EVs, by the turn of the 20th century made up about a third of all cars on the road. These early EVs were all of Lead-Acid type and had the benefit of being very easy to drive. Lead-Acid batteries are heavy but, because EVs were relatively slow, decent range was achieved on a single charge. Recharging a Lead-Acid battery is slow but with the small capacity of the EVs batteries, overnight charging was acceptable. Limited electricity infrastructure, improvements in the 'explosion engine' better known now as the internal combustion engine (ICE), improvements to the road infrastructure inviting longer ranges, faster vehicles, and cheaper mass-produced ICEVs led to the end of the first age of the electric vehicle despite Edison's introduction of a much improved Nickel-Iron (NiFe) battery.

NiFe was developed by Waldemar Jungner in 1899 but was much improved in 1901 by Thomas Edison. It had a much longer life than Lead-Acid and half the recharge time but was more expensive and so made EVs even less competitive with ICEVs.

In the 1960s, whilst some short-range Lead-Acid EVs appeared (Henney Kilowatt, Scamp, and the Enfield 8000) others produced cars with different, albeit unsuccessful, battery technologies. GM's Electrovair used Silver-Zinc (very high energy density but expensive and with low cycle life), and Amitron used an innovative hybrid Lithium Nickel Flouride / NiCd (very high energy density but very poor power release from the Lithium Nickel Flouride was supplemented by the sustained high discharge rate of Nickel-Cadmium NiCd)

Waldemar Junger, the inventor of the Nickel Iron battery also developed the Nickel Cadmium NiCd battery in 1899. As well as high discharge rates without losing capacity they have good low temperature performance and good cycle life but do suffer from 'memory' effect and, as cadmium is highly toxic, cadmium is now banned except in some medical and military applications.

In the 1990s, Lead-Acid, NiCd, and even Ni-Fe batteries were used in some of the few EVs of that generation, (GM EV1 Gen1 and the Ford Ranger EV) but others explored other battery chemistries. The Honda EV+, released in 1988, used NiMH as did the GM EV1 Gen2, Toyota's RAV4 EV and a version of the Ford Ranger. Nickel-Metal Hydride NiMH was developed in 1967 and has a much higher energy density than NiCd. NiMH has a high energy density than NiCd, and a better cycle life and shelf life and gave EVs a credible driving range although recharge time remained quite slow.

Lithium Ion batteries were first proposed by British chemist M Stanley Whittingham during the 1970s whilst working for Exxon but his Lithium-Titanium di-sulphide battery proved to be impractical. Ned Godshall (1979) and separately John Goodenough and Koichi Mizushima (1980) both demonstrated Lithium Cobalt Oxide LCO cells operating in the 4V range

Sony introduced the first commercial Lithium Ion cell in 1991 for use in consumer electronics and it has since displaced many other battery types due to its high cell voltage, its high energy and power density, and today, its ever lower cost.

Nissan produced the first Li-Ion battery powered EV, the Altra, in 1997 and whilst the Gen2 GM1, Toyota RAV4EV and Fords Ranger EV used NiMH, all future EVs were to use variants of the Li-Ion battery. Nissan used Lithium Manganese Oxide - a chemistry they were to carry forward through their early versions of the Leaf range.

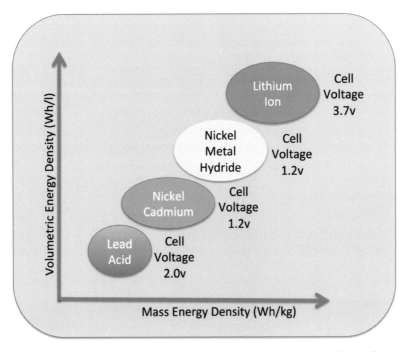

*Lithium Ion Batteries can be significantly smaller and lighter than other rechargeable battery technologies and, importantly, have a much higher nominal cell voltage.*

Lithium is the lightest metal, and the third lightest element; it also has the lowest reduction potential and hence the highest possible cell potential (voltage).

A Lithium-Ion Battery (LIB) has an anode, a cathode, a separator, and an electrolyte. A LIB works by passing lithium ions between the electrodes through an electrolyte solution. As lithium ions move from the anode to the cathode it generates power. For recharging, the lithium ions move from the cathode to the anode.

The Anode is most often Graphite (except LTO) and the Cathode of a mixed metal (NMC, LMO, NCA, etc.). Varying the anode/cathode composition leads to different battery characteristics. The electrolyte is normally a salt - lithium hexaflourophosphate - together with a mix of carbonates.

The separator is either a polymeric membrane, a fabric mat, or sometimes a ceramic.

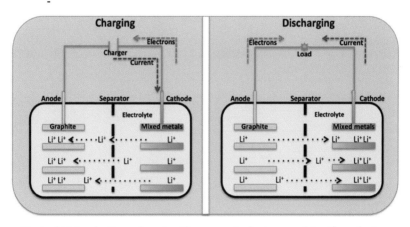

*Typical Li-Ion battery showing the current, electron and Ion flow during charging and discharging.*

The **Solid Electrolyte Interface** SEI is important for any of the LIBS using carbon anodes (most, except LTO). The SEI forms on first use of the battery and prevents the acid electrolyte from dissolving the carbon whilst still allowing ions through. During the life of the battery the SEI will thicken making the ion transfer (intercalation) more difficult and hence reducing the battery capacity. High charge/discharge rates and low temperature charge/discharge will thicken the SEI layer more rapidly.

## Battery Terminology

Rated Capacity, Energy, Energy Density, Specific Energy, C-Rate, State of Charge, State of Health, Depth of Discharge, and Cycle are terms that are commonly used when describing batteries.

**Rated Capacity** – expressed in Amp-hours or Ah and is the current (Amps) that can be delivered continuously from full to empty in a period of one-hour.

**Energy** – is the Rated Capacity at the battery nominal voltage measured in Watt hours or Wh. Watt is a measurement of power and is current multiplied by voltage – Amps x Volts. Nominal voltage is an average voltage over the battery discharge. For example one Amp at two Volts discharged over one hour is 2Wh whereas 2-Amps at 2V over an hour is 4Wh.

**C-rate** – is the rate of discharge related to the rated capacity. So a 10Ah battery at 1C delivers 10A for one-hour whereas a 10Ah battery at 4C delivers 10A for 15 minutes.

**State of Charge** – expressed as a percentage % of the full battery. Often, for the driver's benefit, the %SOC is a % of the net usable capacity rather than the gross capacity.

**Depth of Discharge** – DoD is the difference between the %SOC beginning and %SOC at the end of the discharge prior to recharging.

**Cycle** – is a discharge and recharge to the same SOC. Battery cycle life is the number of cycles from full to empty and back to full. Partial discharge and charge cycles can be summed to make a full cycle.

**State of Health** – is a measure of the current battery capacity compared to the battery capacity when new.

Two other measures are useful when comparing batteries.

**Energy Density** –is the amount of energy within a specific volume of battery.

**Specific Energy** – is the amount of energy within a specific mass (or weight) of battery.

## Li-Ion Battery Chemistry

The principal LIB designations are: LCO, NCA, LMO, NMC, and LFP - these refer to the cathode composition. LTO is the other significant designation. All apart from LTO use a metal or mixed-metal cathode and a graphite anode; LTO uses a metal (titanate) anode and a mixed metal cathode.

For EVs the following spider diagram shows the battery chemistries against five key parameters (5 is best, 1 is worst):

- Energy Density – how much energy (Whs) in a specific space and/or weight.

- Power Density – how quickly the energy can be released.

- Life – how many times it can be cycled.

- Cost – highest score is least expensive.

- Safety – likelihood of a thermal runaway.

- 

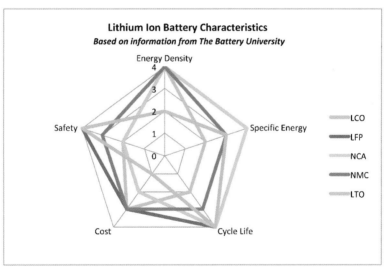

35

## Major LIB Types

- Graphite/Lithium Cobalt Oxide **LCO** is used in most consumer electronics. It has a good cycle life and energy density but poor power density. It is expensive and has a higher likelihood of thermal runaway.

- Graphite/Lithium Iron Phosphate **LFP** has excellent safety and good cycle life but has lower energy and power density as well as a lower cell voltage (3.2V). It has been a favoured technology for 'long-duration between charges' bus and coaches and for marine ferries that can charge only once per day. It also avoids the use of Cobalt.

- Lithium Titanate Oxide/Mixed-Metal **LTO** use a mixed-metal cathode and a titanate metal anode (unlike the other LIB variants) giving it a very fast charge rate, due to the very high surface area from the titanate nano-crystals on the anode and lack of SEI. LTO offers a wide operating temperature and a very high cycle life but a low energy density and a low cell voltage can lead to a high initial battery cost per kWh. LTO is considered very safe and is gaining favour for buses and ferries that are configured to charge very frequently (every hour or sometimes even more frequently).

- Graphite/Lithium Manganese Oxide **LMO** is a safer alternative to LCO but it has a lower cycle life. Nissan's early Leaf used LMO batteries and many EVs adopted a mix of LMO and NMC in their earlier versions for both cost and life reasons.

- Graphite/Nickel Manganese Cobalt **NMC** has become the most widely adopted LIB type for EVs. Early EVs mixed LMO is mixed with NMC - LMO provided the high current boost for acceleration with the NMC providing the longer endurance. Most EV manufacturers now use $NMC_{111}$ with a third of each Ni, Mn and Co. Nickel-Rich NMC reduces the amount of expensive cobalt and in 2018 most EVs have. Nickel rich $NMC_{622.}$ Future cells will see more nickel and less manganese and, importantly for reduced cost, less cobalt. $NMC_{721}$ and $NMC_{811}$, use even less cobalt and these are now being released and can be expected to be in widespread use by 2021/22.

- Graphite/Lithium Nickel Cobalt Aluminium Oxide **NCA** offers a high energy density, a good power density and a long life but has more potential for thermal runaway. NCA's power density is exploited to the full in the Tesla 'Ludicrous' and 'Insane' modes of rapid acceleration.

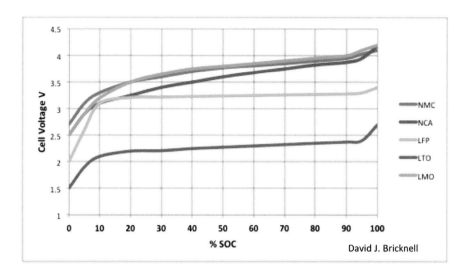

*Illustrative voltage for cell discharge for various cell chemistries.*

*(NMC, NCA and LMO taken from AVT-INL testing. LTO and LFP from The Battery University.)*

## Future LIB developments

Cost, size and recharging time are three of the key areas for battery development.

- Cost can be reduced by scale and also by reducing high-cost minerals, such as Cobalt;

- Size by improving energy density - storing more energy in a given space; and

- Recharging time by improving electrode chemistry to accept charge quicker.

Using **Silicon** together with graphite in the anode significantly improves battery capacity/energy density. Silicon absorbs charge differently from graphite and so designing the battery to cope with the electrode delamination has proved difficult but increasing amounts of silicon are now being integrated into LIBs.

Most EV manufacturers are concentrating on two types of batteries – Tesla - NCA and most others NMC and Nickel-Rich NMC.

Tesla's near term development will involve improved cell chemistry by increasing the amount of silicon into the graphite anode in order to increase energy density. Tesla expects to increase energy density by about 5% each year although some of this will also be down to a nickel-rich NCA.

The NMC users have moved from LMO-NMC to $NMC_{111}$, meaning equal amounts of nickel, manganese and cobalt. Cobalt is by far the most expensive of the constituents for the cathode – it is about 5 times more than nickel and 30 times more than manganese. In order to reduce costs but also to improve performance, the next step is $NMC_{622}$ and $NMC_{721}$, and then to $NMC_{811}$ (80% nickel, 10% manganese and 10% cobalt). The expectations are that $NMC_{811}$ will be introduced between 2018 and 2022, depending upon the supplier.

LG Chem and SK Innovation have indicated their likelihood of bringing $NMC_{811}$ and $NMC_{721}$ to market in 2018 – these are expected in 2019. Samsung SDI has indicated 2021 for BMW. Interestingly LGChem are already using $NMC_{811}$ in cylindrical cells for busses but are retaining $NMC_{622}$ in pouch cells.

Samsung/BMW show their next step (5-years) as $NMC_{811}$ with silicon/graphite anode and then in around 10-years as 'all solid state' electrolyte – each step reducing costs and further improving energy density.

LG Chem are reported to be developing NMCA with added aluminium and reduced cobalt with up to 90% Nickel for around 2022 timescale.

Samsung SDI have are also developing 'Graphene Balls' – such an improvement would mean a doubling on energy density coupled with excellent high and low temperature performance negating the need for a cooling/heating system.

Other longer-term developments include:

Zinc-Air – better known for hearing aids but has the potential as an EV battery

Lithium-Sulphur – a potentially low cost and temperature-tolerant cell but one that has yet to be successfully developed

Lithium-Air –offering potentially 5-10 times the energy density of today's batteries but is at the beginning of its development. Jaguar Land Rover are associated with Johnson Matthey Battery Systems as an end-user to investigate how Lithium Air cells can be integrated into automotive applications, achieving initially specific energy of around 400Wh/kg

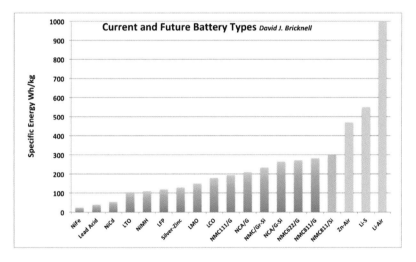

One significant development eagerly anticipated for some time is the solid-state LIB where the liquid electrolyte is replaced with a solid ceramic electrolyte. Solid State LIBS will be more energy dense, maybe two to three times higher.

A key characteristic is the lack of an SEI so charging rates can be higher and cycle life longer. Seeo/Bosch, Dyson/Sakti, Fisker, Toyota, VW/Quantumscape and BMW/Solid Power are all working to commercialise solid-state batteries by the early 2020s.

## Battery Life

**Battery Cell Life** is a combination of **Calendar life** and **Cycle life**:

**Calendar Life** is influenced by temperature, maximum cell voltage, and time.

Cell resistance increases with:

- elapsed time, due to a build up of a passivation layer of unwanted chemicals on the anode; the speed with which resistance increases is greater at higher temperatures.

- higher cell voltages, even if only achieved briefly, will increase calendar ageing and reduce cycle life.

- higher charge rates increase the loss of lithium to the Solid Electrolyte Interface SEI layer (except LTO). Initially the SEI forms and protects the electrode from the electrolyte but the SEI will thicken over time hastening the loss of capacity. Lithium plating occurs at very high charge rates.

**Cycle Life** is normally described as the number of complete charge and discharge cycles it can sustain before its nominal 80% capacity is exceeded. One cycle is a complete charge and discharge. Five partial 20% charge and discharges is equal to one cycle. Battery life reduces with increasing number of cycles.

Cycle life varies with varying electrode chemistries and with rate and Depth of Discharge (DOD): the amount of active chemicals transformed during charge and discharge is broadly proportional to the DOD.

For the same EV, the DOD per cell is lower on larger capacity battery packs for the same journey. For the 20kWh ~ 80 mile range per charge, 1000 full cycles corresponds to 80,000 – 118,000 miles which at an average 10,000 to 12,000 miles per annum equates to about eight years. For a 60kWh 240mile battery pack, the same annual mileage is only a third of the cycle life, albeit the larger battery capacity may well encourage longer and faster road trips incurring higher-C-rates and probably higher DODs.

The Rate of Charge and of Discharge (C-Rate) affects battery life as the chemical processes that take place during discharge will be less complete the more rapidly it occurs.

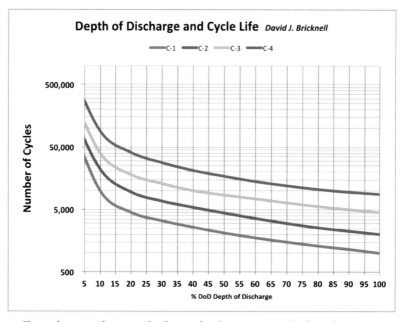

*Chart showing the typical relationship between Depth of Discharge and number of cycles for different rates of discharge.*

## Cell Voltage and Cell Capacity -

As the cell discharges the voltage reduces from its maximum until it reaches the minimum operating voltage. The maximum for todays LIB is usually between 4.1 and 4.2V and the minimum around 3.4-3.5V: the minimum operating voltage is some way above the minimum cell voltage - the rather steep reduction in cell voltage that can be seen in the chart below as the cell nears complete discharge discourages further discharge.

As the cell ages and as cycling reduces its capacity the shape of the discharge curve remains the same but the Capacity Ah reduces, as can be seen in the graph below

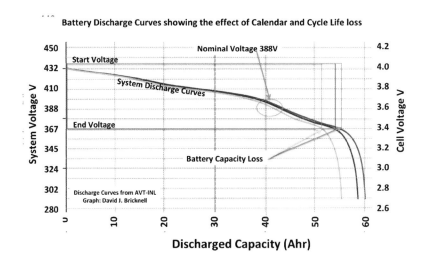

Chemical reactions within the battery cell are affected by **cell voltage** and **battery temperature**:

**Cell Voltage** - Once all the available chemical reactions within a cell have been completed and it has reached its upper cell voltage, then forcing more energy into a cell will cause it to heat up whilst producing irreversible chemical reactions that will damage the cell. Similar irreversible reactions occur when discharging the cell below its lower voltage limit.

## Temperature of Operation –

The hotter the battery, the faster the internal chemical reactions will be. Higher temperatures will mean higher power but also a shorter life.

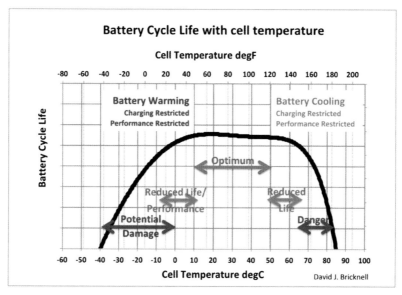

*Batteries have an optimum operating temperature. Operating outside of this can lead to reduced cycle life and to performance degradation.*

As an illustration of the battery cell temperature strategies deployed by EV suppliers:

BMW uses battery heating as part of their preconditioning process bringing the battery cell temperatures to 10°C (50°F) – there is some range benefits to this but preserving battery cycle life is the biggest benefit.

BMW restricts regeneration below 10°C (50°F) and Tesla prevents regeneration below zero C (32°F), other manufacturers will have similar battery strategies.

BMW prevents rapid charging in cells exceeding 50°C (120°F).

Jaguar will be using similar strategies for the I-Pace.

## Battery usable capacity varies with cell temperature and discharge rate

As the battery cell temperature drops, due to reduced ambient temperature, the usable battery capacity reduces. This means that some of the energy charged into the battery cannot be accessed.

This chart shows the reduction in cell capacity (at a 1-C discharge rate) with reducing cell temperature for a generic NMC LIB.

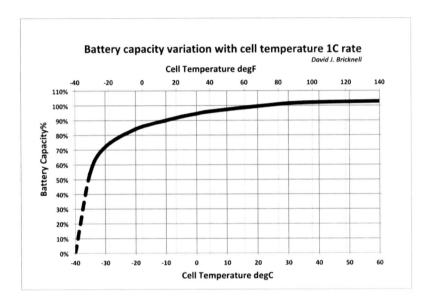

EVs generally offer three strategies for protecting against the impact of lower cell temperatures

- preconditioning of the battery to about 10°C – this usually takes a few hours due to the high thermal mass of the cells; too rapid heating will likely distort the cell.

- power restriction, reducing the available discharge rate (power and acceleration).

- Charging rate restriction / battery cell heating

## Discharge/Charge Rate C-Rate

The battery C-Rate is a term expressing how quickly the battery is discharging energy compared to the total battery capacity per hour.

Lithium-Ion cells show a reduction in cell voltage as the cells discharge. The rate at which the cell voltage reduces is affected by the rate at which the discharge occurs – higher rates of power will more rapidly reduce the cell voltage in turn reducing the capacity of the cell.

Similarly higher charge rates will more quickly increase cell voltage – one of the reasons for slowing charge rate when nearing high SOC.

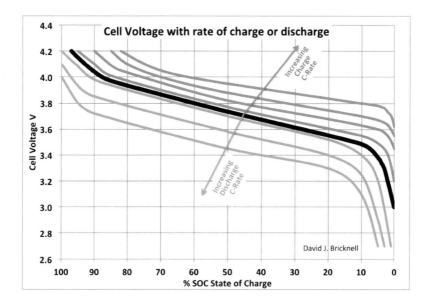

## Cell and System Voltage in operation

Cell and System Voltage will vary considerable over the driving cycle depending upon the nature of the drive – urban, highway/motorway and whether the drive is aggressive in nature or not.

The chart below shows a typical EV (NMC battery) driven over a variety of standard driving cycles including an aggressive cycle. This chart shows the drive at a cold -4°C/25°F and demonstrates the wide divergence from a smooth static capacity discharge. In this case the BMS has a set system 395V / cell 4.1V upper and 330V / 3.4V lower limit

During operation, particularly under acceleration, the instantaneous cell voltage will drop below 3.4V - during a similar test at -4degC the cell voltage can be seen as instantaneously low as 3.23V (system 310V) and during similar tests at -17degC cell voltages as low as 2.9V (system 280V) can be seen. The car's management system will seek to avoid the cell voltage dropping too low and will restrict power if such an event seems likely.

**Driving Cycle at -4°C  -  Energy discharged over driving cycles  17.47kWhrs**

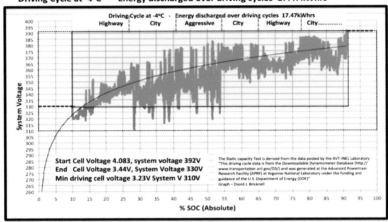

## Usable Battery Capacity

Usable battery capacity will vary with a combination of cell temperature and discharge rate.

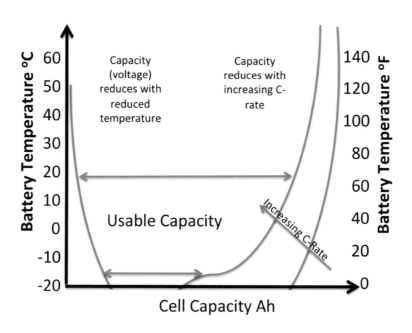

*For the EV LIB the above graph illustrates the 'full' battery reducing as cell temperature falls – around 10% loss from 30ºC to 0ºC. More dramatic, however, is the effect of discharge rate at lower temperatures where high discharge rates (rapid acceleration and high-speeds) will reduce the effective battery capacity substantially due to rapid internal cell heating.*

## Battery Formats

Three shapes of LIBs, pouch, and cylindrical and prismatic, are used in current EVs with each having their own strengths:

**Pouch**, used by Jaguar and also by Nissan, Renault, GM, VW, Hyundai, and others allows a very flat and thin installation. The electrodes are bonded together with a polymer that also acts as the separator. The electrolyte is infused into the polymer and becomes a gel meaning that the battery can be packaged in a foil envelope instead of a solid case. The foil envelopes are then packed into a module and the modules stacked within the overall battery pack. Pouch cells are also known as LiPo or Lithium Polymer. Minimal cell packaging should lead to a higher energy density although some structure is essential to contain and constrain the pouches. Pouches tend to be large slim and envelope-shaped which can present a large surface area for cooling. Pouches can be stacked flat or on edge, those on edge are tending towards very wide and very short, almost a strip-like letter-box format, minimizing cabin intrusion.

*Wide format LG Chem NMC Cell and the packaging within the Jaguar I-Pace battery pack. Jaguar has 36 modules per pack with 12 cells per module. I-Pace picture courtesy of Halit Murat Gültekin*

**Cylindrical** - The cylindrical battery is like a Swiss-roll or jelly-roll of positive electrode (normally a copper foil base), separator, negative electrode (normally an aluminium foil base) and separator rolled up. Anode and Cathode materials are coated onto the metal foils. Tesla is the principal EV proponent of cylindrical cells although the configuration has widespread usage outside of EVs. Lucid Motors and Faraday Future are also likely to adopt this format should they eventually bring their EVs to market.

Most popular cylindrical size is the 18650 (18mm in diameter and 65mm in length) although 20700, 21700, and 26650 are also available. The latest Tesla-Panasonic uses a 21700 size, although they refer to it as 2170. Samsung has recently produced a modular 2170 pack in a similar format to prismatic but with twice the prismatic cell's energy density.

Cylindrical cells do seem to offer very high packing densities and, because of the small cell energy, offer more flexibility to vary battery pack capacity.

*The Tesla Model S 100D uses 8,256 of the 18650 format NCA cells in its battery pack. Photo courtesy of Oleg Alexandrov (cc-by-sa-3.0)*

**Prismatic** Prismatic cells use layers of anode, separator, cathode, separator, etc., within a hard aluminium case. The electrodes and separators are wound, as a flattened spiral, or stacked as sheets giving a lower density pack size than the cylindrical arrangement.

Significantly less cells are normally used in prismatic battery packs compared to cylindrical or pouch as the cell Amp-hours can be much greater e.g. Samsung SDI has 26, 28, 60, 94, and 120Ah available.

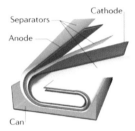

*Typical construction of a prismatic battery cell.*

*Samsung SDI Prismatic NMC cells within an i3 module package. Photo courtesy of Gonville Bromhead*

This page intentionally blank

# Pack configurations

Within the battery pack the cells can be connected in series, in parallel or in a combination of both.

Serial connection determines the battery pack voltage – add the voltages of each cell together.

Parallel connection adds the current of the batteries together but holds to the cell voltage.

EV manufacturers use various combinations of serial and parallel configurations.

| EV | Cell | Parallel | Series | No. of cells | Cell Voltage Nominal V | Cell Capacity Ah | Battery Energy Ah | System Voltage, nom | kWh (gross) | Source |
|---|---|---|---|---|---|---|---|---|---|---|
| **Pouch (Li-Po)** | | | | | | | | | | |
| GM Bolt/Ampera-E | LG Chem | 3 | 96 | 288 | 3.65 | 57.1 | 171 | 350 | 60.0 | EPA submission |
| Hyundai Ioniq | LG Chem | 1 | 96 | 96 | 3.75 | 78.0 | 78 | 360 | 28.1 | EPA submission |
| Hyundai Kona 64 | LG-Chem | 3 | 98 | 294 | 3.63 | 60.0 | 180 | 356 | 64.1 | EPA submission |
| Hyundai Kona 39.2 | LG-Chem | 2 | 90 | 180 | 3.63 | 60.0 | 120 | 327 | 39.2 | |
| Jaguar i-Pace | LG-Chem | 4 | 108 | 432 | 3.59 | 55.7 | 223 | 388 | 86.5 | EPA submission |
| Kia Soul | SK Innovation | 2 | 100 | 200 | 3.60 | 40.0 | 80 | 360 | 28.8 | EPA submission |
| Kia Niro | SK Innovation | 3 | 98 | 294 | 3.63 | 60.0 | 180 | 356 | 64.1 | EPA submission |
| Nissan Leaf 40 | AESC | 2 | 96 | 192 | 3.65 | 57.5 | 115 | 350 | 40.3 | EPA submission |
| Renault Zoe 40 | LG Chem | 2 | 96 | 192 | 3.75 | 65.0 | 130 | 360 | 46.8 | EPA submission |
| VW e-Golf | Panasonic | 3 | 88 | 264 | 3.67 | 37.0 | 111 | 323 | 35.9 | EPA submission |
| **Cylindrical** | | | | | | | | | | |
| Tesla S/X P100D | Tesla-Panasonic | 89 | 96 | 8544 | 3.65 | 3.1 | 279 | 350 | 97.8 | |
| Tesla 3 LR | Tesla-Panasonic | 42 | 96 | 4032 | 3.65 | 5.5 | 230 | 350 | 80.5 | EPA submission |
| **Prismatic** | | | | | | | | | | |
| BMW i3 120Ah | Samsung SDI | 1 | 96 | 96 | 3.70 | 120.0 | 120 | 352 | 42.2 | EPA submission |

Clearly the building blocks of each cell will impact on the configuration of the battery pack. Most EVs have, until recently, used 96 cells in series but different numbers in parallel. Hyundai/Kia have extended the number in series to 98 and 100 but the I-Pace is the first to use 108 although they are soon to be followed by the Audi e-Tron. Using 96 cells leads to pack voltage of approximately a nominal 350V and max 400, whereas 108 cells will be a nominal of 388 and a max of 450V

The i3 uses all cells in series in order to reach the required system voltage. The Leaf with cells of just over half the energy (Ah) of the i3 reaches system voltage with the same number of cells but needs twice as many in order to provide the required system energy. The Bolt uses three times as many cells of similar energy to the i3 in order to achieve a battery pack three times the capacity. Tesla uses the 18650 and 21700 cylindrical cells; it needs 96 cells in series to reach system voltage and, for the S85, 74 in parallel to reach battery energy capacity. The more circuits in parallel, the more modular the battery pack can be whilst holding to a common system voltage.

An 800V system will have twice the number of cells in series.

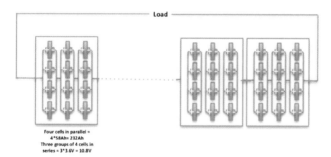

Four cells in parallel =
4*58Ah≈ 232Ah
Three groups of 4 cells in
series = 3*3.6V = 10.8V

36 modules including 12 Cells. 4 in parallel and three groups of 4 cells in series

36 modules * 223Ah * 10.8V = 86.7kWh

108 groups of four cells in series - 108* 3.6V = 388V nominal

Parallel connection of multiple series connected battery cells is required when the current available from individual cells is insufficient for the required power or increasing the number in series lead to too high a system voltage.

For light commercial vehicles and for marine installations system voltages are more often greater than 700V with some exceeding one kV.

## Battery Temperature Management

Different cell chemistries will have differing operational temperatures.

For the mixed-metal-graphite cells (LFP, LMO, NMC and NCA) an operational cell temperature range of -40°C to +50°C (-40°F to 120°F) is typical – note: not ambient temperature but cell temperature, cells being quite slow to respond to ambient temperature changes.

However, at cell temperatures below zeroC (32F) the significant increase in cell internal resistance will reduce the performance of mixed metal–graphite LIBs on discharge rate, to avoid excessive internal heating, and on charge rate so much so that manufacturers will prevent charging until cells have been heated to above zeroC in order to avoid lithium plating on the anode leading to reduced battery cycle life.

The optimum cell temperature for performance and life is 25°C to 40°C

EVs have adopted one of three cooling strategies broadly depending upon cell type.

Pouch Cells are cooled either by forced air, by water glycol coolant or by a water-glycol/refrigerant mix.

- Hyundai Ioniq, Kia Soul, Renault Zoe and VW e-Golf all use a forced air-cooling system, in which the battery pack is force ventilated with ambient air using a fan. Kia has linked their system to the cooling or heating of cabin air.

- GM Bolt/Ampera-E uses a water glycol coolant circulated through a bottom plate within the battery pack and thin passive cooling fins between the pouch cells – this is not the same as with the Volt as there is no intra-cell active fin cooling plate, something that was probably necessary for a PHEV and not for a BEV.

- Jaguar I-Pace, Hyundai Kona and Kia e-Niro use a water-glycol mix coolant for lower temperatures but bring in refrigerant cooling when cell temperatures rise. A resistive element or/and heat pump is used for cell heating.

Tesla's Cylindrical Cells are cooled by water glycol coolant circulated between the rows of cells. A chiller is also to reduce liquid coolant temperature as necessary and in the Tesla S&X an in-line heating element raises cell temperature when required although cell heating can also be done by activating the motor at zero rpm drawing power from the cells and hence self-heating – in this manner cell heating of the cell is from the inside and not from the outside.

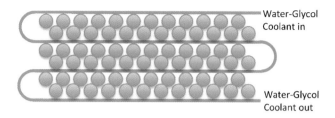

Water-Glycol
Coolant in

Water-Glycol
Coolant out

BMW's Prismatic Cells are cooled by a refrigerant in tubes running underneath the prismatic cell modules. Contained within the battery-pack is the refrigerant cooling system that is shared with the air conditioning system.

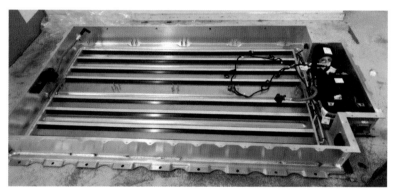

*BMW i3 battery pack casing showing the cooling tubes running along the bottom of the casing. Photo courtesy Philip Ivanier*

A battery pack resistive heater of is fitted to pre-condition the battery pack during spells of cold weather. The pre-conditioning warms the battery cells to about 10ᵒC / 50ᵒF in order to minimize cycle-life loss and to allow recuperation of energy.

# Preconditioning of battery

Low battery cell temperatures reduce available capacity and available power, will limit energy regeneration, impact on battery life, and will increase recharge time.

Preconditioning or heating of battery is done slowly to ensure that cells are warmed evenly and don't distort. The aim of preconditioning is to bring the battery to a temperature of about 10°C / 50°F.

A graph of the preconditioning process shows packets of heating being applied and this then being allowed to soak through before the next heating input. LIBs have a high thermal mass and are slow to warm and to cool; too much heat too quickly will lead to physical cell distortion.

This chart shows a typical preconditioning process.

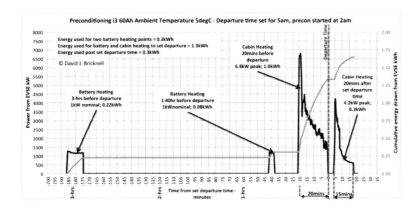

*Typical preconditioning power and energy usage showing the early discrete packages of energy applied to heat the battery and then to let it soak through.*

## Battery Management System

The BMS has a key safety role in ensuring that the maximum cell voltage does not exceed the level where thermal runaway might occur; this can be as little as a few hundred millivolts over the maximum. Overvoltage, even by a little, can also significantly affect cell degradation and critically shorten battery life.

The BMS ensures that a uniform charge is provided to the HV battery. It measures the:

- system voltage,
- current flowing into or out from,
- individual cell voltages and temperatures, and
- calculates the State of Charge (SOC) and
- calculates the State of Health (SOH).

During charging, the BMS signals the cell voltage and temperature, (typically every tenth of a second), and, taking this into account, it demands the right level of current to be delivered by the charger.

The CSSU monitors every battery cell for cell voltage and temperature (cells differ due to manufacturing tolerances and ageing) and communicates with the BMS to adjust the charging and balance the cells for optimum performance.

The BMS will also protect against over-discharge, the point where all lithium ions are removed from the graphite anode. This would lead to excessive corrosion and prevent further operation of the cell.

The State of Charge for an EV is the actual calculated battery capacity at that moment compared to the maximum usable battery capacity: battery capacity for a LIB varies with cell temperature, the rate of charge and discharge, and the time between charges.

Measuring a battery's SOC to a specific accuracy (current to an accuracy of $\pm0.5\%$ and voltage to an accuracy of better than $\pm0.1\%$) necessary for an EV is quite difficult. EV batteries are normally sampled by the BMS between 20 and 100 times per second.

# Battery Cell balancing

Ensuring that the 108 cells in series are balanced in order to avoid overcharging individual cells and to maximise battery capacity is a challenge: cells at the beginning of life have normal manufacturing variation and through life the imbalance can worsen if not managed.

During charging the strongest cell will reach full first, leaving the weakest short of charge whilst during discharge the weakest cell is then depleted first meaning the fullest charged cells are never fully discharged. The total battery capacity is thus reduced and this will worsen if not addressed.

Two different strategies can be adopted to resolve battery cell imbalance and to increase battery pack life and capacity: one is passive balancing and the other active balancing, albeit there are variations on each type.

Passive balancing reduces the energy in the most charged cell and dissipates it through a resistor allowing the other cells to catch up; it is only done whilst charging or resting but not during discharging.

Active balancing takes the extra energy from the highest charged cells and transfers it to the cells least charged; it can be implemented during charging and discharging.

Most of today's EVs adopt passive balancing as it is relatively simple, is inexpensive, and well suited to smaller battery packs. Active balancing, implemented during charge and discharge, is more complex, more expensive, but is better suited to larger battery packs where charging to full is likely to be less frequent and to PHEV batteries which are rarely fully charged.

To passive balance, the cells, charge to 90% and leave plugged in – this will trigger the balancing process. Do this regularly and the cells will be kept in a good state of balance.

**Passive cell balancing** will, once the first cell in the battery module or pack is fully charged, dissipate the energy from the highest charged cells through a resistor as heat. At the next charging session the lower charged cells can then catch up at the next charging session.

The gap between the usable and gross battery capacity is used for passive balancing the battery as well as for maintaining the life of the battery.

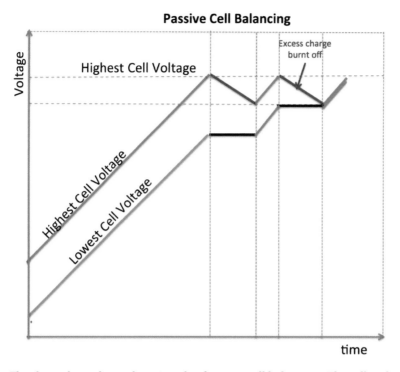

## Passive Cell Balancing

*The chart above shows the principle of passive cell balancing. The cell with the highest voltage determines the point to stop charging. Once stopped the Cell Supervision Unit burns off the extra charge through a small resistor, hence the process may take some time after charging ends. With some Passive Systems, charging may restart and stop again to balance all the cells whilst others will use the next charge cycle, or preconditioning, to top up the cells again.*

**Active cell balancing** uses either capacitive, inductive charge or, for faster balancing, power converter/PWM to distribute energy from the higher charged cells and provide it to the lower charged cells: this avoids the energy losses that are incurred by passive balancing.

Active balancing can be done whilst the cells are charging or discharging however the ability to balance is reduced as charge or discharge rate goes up, so if your EV uses active balancing either drive more slowly occasionally or recharge on a lower powered charger every now and again.

Active balancing is well suited to larger battery packs and PHEV batteries and is preferable for energy reasons although the extra complexity comes at a cost.

This page intentionally blank

# Charging

## Overview

Charging (and re-charging on-route or at a destination) is something new to drivers of ICE vehicles and, as with all newly introduced technologies, there are a myriad of different charging plugs, charging rates, charging companies and charging standards.

This section looks at the principles of charging, rates of charge and discharge, charging efficiency, the effects of charging on the battery (including heating and battery life), and State of Charge (SOC) (how it's measured and what it means) and the effects on charging speed of cell temperature.

National and International charging infrastructures are rapidly developing and expanding but for the moment there are many different charging companies and a multitude of different cost models – things will no doubt get clearer as the technology settles down.

The latest models of EV with larger capacity battery packs will mean, for some drivers, very little charging away from home, perhaps none at all for some. For the high-mileage traveller and for the once or twice a year vacation traveller, access to on-route rapid chargers is essential and here the power available at the charger is beginning to increase (50 to 150 and on to 350kW) to cover the higher capacity battery packs, not forgetting, of course, that for many a rapid charge may entail only just enough energy to complete the journey.

A number of manufacturers have discussed 800V electrical systems for EVs - essentially 192 to 216 cells in series for todays LIBs. Should such systems be introduced then charge time will reduce along with size and weight of the on board electrics with the charge being completed at home.

For the I-Pace charging includes DC CCS2.0 at a maximum of 240A or 100kW max before charge rate is reduced by BMS) or CCS1.0 at 200A or approx. 83kW. AC charging is at 32A/7kW.

Manufacturers charging times AC

Charging 0-100% on AC 7kW/32A  12.9hrs

Charging 0-80% on  AC 7kW/32A  10.0hrs

Charging 0-80% on  DC CCS1.0   40mins

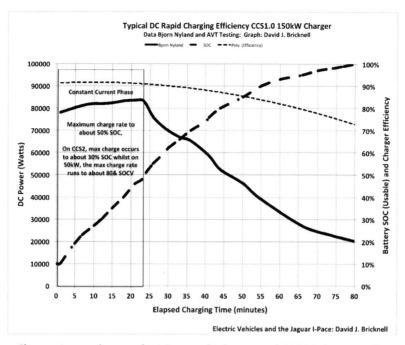

*Charge time and power for I-Pace on high-powered CCS1.0 charger. Also shown is a typical DC Charger efficiency although this will depend on configuration of power electronics.*

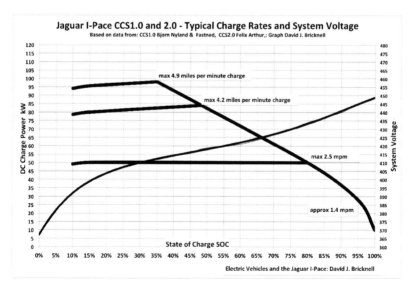

*I-Pace charge profiles against State-of-Charge on CCS2.0 charge levels, CCS1.0 high-powered charger, and on the ubiquitous 50kW CCS.*

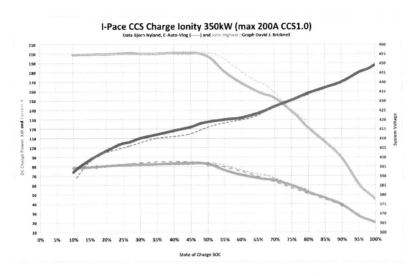

*This chart shows power kW, Current Amps, and System Voltage all against State of Charge. The I-Pace seems unusual in completing the constant current phase at 420V/3.88V before maximum cell voltage 450V/4.17V is achieved – cell voltage continues to rise whilst charge current is declining.*

*Jaguar I-Pace on a Mode 3 charger. Photograph courtesy Daniel F. Bohmer*

Mode 4 charging at an on-route CCS. Rapid chargers are essential for timely longer journeys. *Photograph courtesy Daniel F. Bohmer*

## Charging Li-Ion Batteries

The charging rate for Lithium Ion Batteries (LIBs) is dependent upon how quickly the chemical reactions can take place within the cell and this is influenced by:

- The rate of chemical reaction of the electrode with the electrolyte,

- The speed at which the electrode surface can move on to the next chemical reaction,

- The speed with which Lithium Ions can be inserted into the host electrode.

These three processes are temperature dependent with colder batteries requiring a longer time both to charge and to discharge:

- Too rapid a discharge can lead to cracking or crystal growth in the electrodes.

- Too rapid a charge will force too much current through the battery which can result in surplus ions being deposited irreversibly on the anode in the form of lithium metal (lithium plating).

EVs carefully control the rate of charge and discharge. LIBs adopt a constant-current / constant-voltage charge system and hence any charging system must be able to monitor and control both current and voltage: LIBs can be damaged if the upper voltage limit is exceeded.

During the constant current CC phase the charging current is at the maximum that the charger can provide, subject to any other maximum imposed by the manufacturer. Power will increase as voltage increases until the cell voltage nears its maximum after which the charger switches to a constant voltage CV mode. During the constant voltage phase, the current will initially decrease rapidly and then more gradually until, at a pre-determined point (typically <3% of rated current), full-charge is reached and the charge is abruptly stopped. The current at the cut off will be dependent on the battery pack size: a 90kWh pack completing its charge at 4.5 times the current (same cell voltage) as that of a similar 20kWh pack.

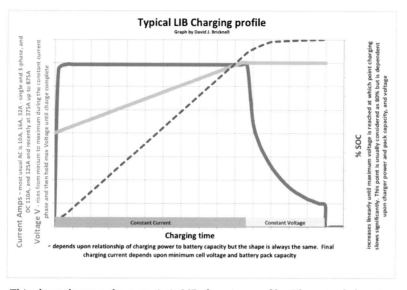

*This chart shows a characteristic LIB charging profile. The actual charging time will depend on the charger power and the battery pack capacity and system voltage.*

## Charging Rate

Charging rate is important to the cycle life of the battery. Charging rate is expressed as C-Rate. This is the charging power related to the battery capacity – a 1-C rate for a 20kWh battery is 20kW and for a 90kWh battery is 90kW. As can be seen from the chart below up to 1.5-C is relatively benign (~135kW for the I-Pace) and 2-C (~180kW) probably acceptable for occasional charging. Charging beyond 2-C will inevitably deteriorate the battery SOH rapidly.

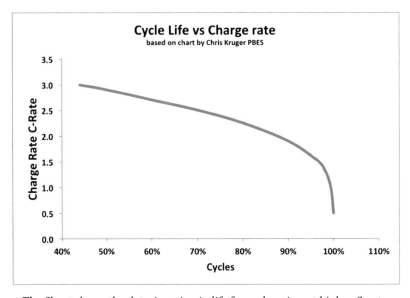

*The Chart shows the deterioration in life from charging at higher C-rates (this is for LIBs with graphite anodes and excludes LTO and solid-state).*

Today's 50kW rapid chargers are within 2-C for most of the current EVs but as charger power increases to 150 then to 350kW the limitation of 2-C charge rate may not then result in quicker charges unless battery capacities increase significantly. On CCS1.0 Jaguar has a max charge rate of about 1-C (84kW on a battery capacity of 90kWh). On CCS2.0 the charge rate is expected to be just over 1-C.

## Charging Modes

The EV battery pack is always charged with Direct Current (DC) with the conversion from Alternating Current (AC) to DC being done either within the EV or on the off-car charger.

In Europe, the modes of charging for EVs are defined in IEC 61851 and plugs, sockets, connectors and cable assemblies are defined in IEC 62196.

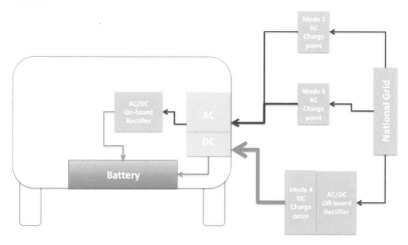

In Modes 1, 2, and 3 the conversion from AC to DC is done within the vehicle. In Mode 4, the conversion of AC to DC is done in the off-car charging unit and bypasses the AC/DC rectifiers in the vehicle – this minimises both the size of the on-car AC/DC rectifiers (and their subsequent inefficiency at lower power) and the impact on the on-board vehicle's cooling system.

**Mode 1** (up to 16A per phase) is not often used because of the lack of communication between the vehicle and the voltage supply.

**Mode 2** (up to 32A per phase) is used from a non-dedicated power supply such as a domestic power socket. The control and protection device is integrated into the charging cable and the charger (AC-DC rectifier) is in the vehicle.

*Mode 2 Charger for slow-speed charging*

**Mode 3** Either 230V 1-phase (up to 16kW/70A) or 400V 3-phase (up to 44kW/63A) supply is used from a dedicated EV charging station either installed at home or on route. The control, communication and protection functions are all integrated into the charge point with the charger device (AC-DC rectifier) being in the vehicle. Most EV drivers have a Mode 3 domestic charge point installed at 32A/7.4kW (230V).

*Mode 3 dedicated EVSE*

The charge cable can be separate or tethered to the EVSE as a user option.

For Mode 2 and 3, charging utilises on-board AC/DC rectifier(s); these are usually optimised around 16A and 32A single phase and 3-phase meaning 3.7kW, 7.4kW, and 11 kW and 22kW for 3-phase. Some EVs charge at up to 43kW AC.

The Jaguar I-Pace charges single-phase AC at up to 32A as do almost all other EVs.

BMW's i3 also includes 32A by using two 16A rectifiers. Later models have added a third 16A rectifier to enable three simultaneous charges at 16A or 48A/11kW on three phase supplies

Depending on the market, the Tesla Models S&X have either one or two on board rectifiers each at 40A/10kW for 230V input. 80A/20kW is available if two on-board chargers are included. Or a 32A/7.4kW charger for the UK and some other markets. Tesla's Model 3 has a 48A/11kW capability at 230V.

**Mode 4 DC Charging**. Mode 4 is a dedicated DC rapid charging from an external charger. Rapid charging EVSEs use AC electricity from the grid and convert it to DC in the charging unit before it gets to the vehicle.

Currently there are two competing open rapid charge systems available - CCS, and CHAdeMO, and one proprietary - Tesla Super Charger. There is also one used solely in China - GB/T 20234.3-2011 DC although China has now signaled that they will adopt CHAdeMO.

**CHAdeMO** – developed by Nissan and Mitsubishi in 2010 (together with Tokyo Electric Power Company and Fuji Heavy Industries) with Toyota joining the standard later. CHAdeMO can deliver up to 50kW and 120A at up to 500V DC. A 150kW version was announced in 2017.

**CCS system** – developed by the majority of European and US car manufacturers and supported by SAE and ACEA with the aim of developing a single and open global standard. CCS combines single and three-phase AC charging up to 44kW as well as DC charging up to 200kW and most recently up to 350kW. Most DC CCS chargers found today offer a range of power with 20, 44, 48 or 50kW but 150kW, 175kW and 350kW units are becoming available.

A number of consortia of EV and equipment manufacturers (Ultra E, Efacec, Porsche, etc.) has begun rolling out 350kW CCS charging units in the expectation that by 2018 some EVs will be capable of charging at that power level. For very high charging rates both connector and cable require active cooling.

Most of today's (2018) EVs are capable of charging at 50kW, except the e-Golf at 40kW. Many are capable beyond 50kW on CCS1.0 and others at a higher level again on the CCS2.0 standard – Ioniq at 70kW and Kona and e-Niro at 77kW.

The I-Pace  charges at up to 84kW on CCS1.0 rapid chargers and around 95kW on CCS2.0.

Two of its closest competitors are anticipated to charge at 110kW (EQC) and 150kW (E-Tron). Tesla superchargers are capable of charging S&X at up to 145kW although currently the 75 model can achieve 100kW and the 100 models just short of 120kW. The Model 3 looks capable of 200kW with EPA documentation stating charge power of up to 525A).

Most of today's vehicles use a 400V system voltage although more and more models are increasing this to around 410V to 420V - both the I-Pace and E-Tron are using 450V).

When the EVSE is connected to the EV the charger detects the connection and then signals to the EV that the DC circuit has been made. The EV's Battery Management System BMS responds with its charge level, battery voltage, and the current the battery can accept.  Charging is managed by the external charger and is based on data communicated by the EV.

The BMS communicates with the Rapid Charger EVSE to control voltage and current during charging, constantly identifying the state of charge and monitoring all sensor signals of the high-voltage battery including temperature. In order to ensure optimal progress of the charging procedure, the BMS calculates current values for the maximum charging power based on these values and communicates these every tenth of a second.

The BMS controls heating/cooling of the high-voltage battery throughout the charging procedure.  This contributes to a quick and efficient charging procedure. Safety functions for isolating the battery are also contained in the BMS.

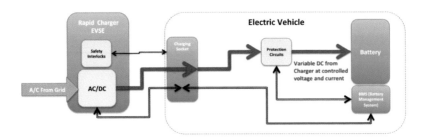

## Charging times when increasing charge power

Charge Time for different battery pack sized from increasing charge power, assuming 400V system Voltage. At 450V the charge should be a little quicker if maximum current coincided with maximum voltage but this is not the case with the I-Pace which has a system voltage of just short of 420V at maximum charging current).

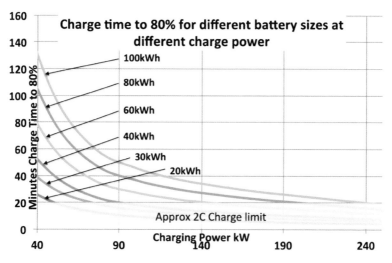

*DC charging time depends upon battery size and charging power. Many of today's chargers are 50kW continuous (125A) into a 400V battery pack although some are restricted 44kW continuous (110A). Into the 420V max of the I-Pace a charge power of 52.5kW is achievable and on higher power CCS1.0 84Kw with CCS2.0 (150kW, 175kW and 350kW) expecting around 95kW.*

## Efficiency of Charging

The efficiency of the charging process will vary between chargers and between charging modes.

The chart below illustrates the different efficiency of a single 16A and twin 16A on-board rectifiers as well as a typical '50kw' DC charger when delivering energy into a LIB battery pack.

Clearly from this graph it is extremely inefficient to use a high-powered DC charger to deliver low power as a large proportion of the electricity taken from the grid will be dissipated as heat. This is also true of using the lower powered rectifiers at very low powers.

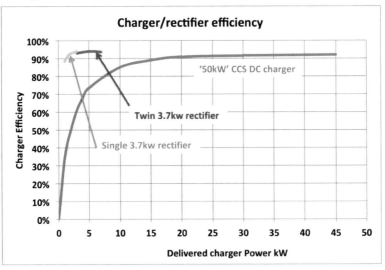

# Charging rates and profiles – AC Fast and DC Rapid

### Mode 3 Fast Charging

Mode 3 AC Charging depends upon the rectifier efficiency within the EV. The I-Pace has a 32A/7kW @ 230V capability.

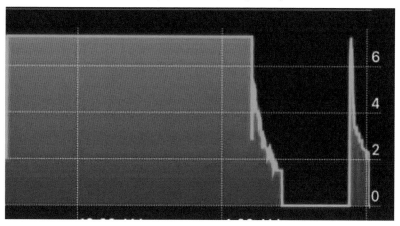

*Chart showing a typical 7kW/32A/230V charge showing the distinctive CC-CV charging profile. Energy is quickly gained during the Constant Current phase and then the charge slowly completes in the Constant Voltage phase – think of it as filling a glass of Prosecco. The end cut-off charge is sharp and relates to the maximum cell voltage – the greater the capacity of the battery the higher the cut-off charge but the cut-off voltage remains the same – for the I-Pace this looks to be about 1.75kW when on a 7kW/32A charger.*

*The scale on the right hand side is kW and along the bottom is time – for this charge the main vertical grid line is at 4-hour intervals.*

*Also shown on the chart is the next morning's cabin precondition spike.*

*Chart courtesy of John Higham.*

### Mode 4 DC Rapid Charging

Mode 4 DC rapid Charging depends on the rectifier efficiency in the off-board charging unit but typically this will be >93% (manufacturers' claim) at peak current but will reduce at lower power levels.

## Temperature - AC Charging

When charging at AC, there are rectifier losses as well as the round-trip battery charging/discharging losses. The chart below is indicative of the losses expected through the ambient temperature range for todays EVs.

EVs can vary considerable with rectifier efficiency with some models being as low as 80% - some very early EVs showed rectifier inefficiencies as low as 65%.

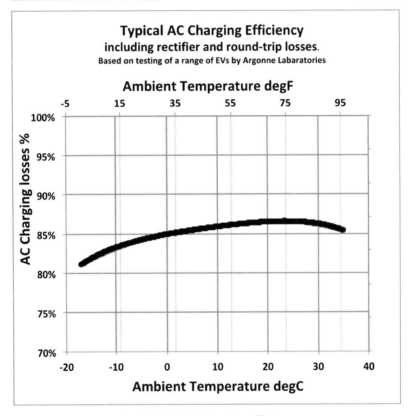

*Typical 32A AC charging efficiency*
*- indicating losses for rectifier and for round trip battery losses.*

## Temperature - DC Charging

AVT-INEL conducted a series of tests on a number of EVs including BMW i3, Nissan Leaf and VW e-Golf. This measured the rate of charge, the rate and total amount of energy taken by the battery, and the battery pack temperature rise. There were differences between these EVs that can be attributed to cell chemistry and battery pack heating and cooling.

However, consistently at the lower temperature the charge is, for a large part, if not all, delivered at around half the power of the higher temperature the consequence of which is that the 80% charge takes around twice as long: something to be aware of when paying for time-based charging.

Overall the energy taken for the full charge is around 5% greater at the higher ambient temperature due to battery pack cooling load.

Battery cell temperature rose more at the lower temperature charge mostly due to the longer charge time.

Reports on cold weather performance of the I-Pace are that the charge takes a while to gain power but does peak at maximum power albeit very briefly. Charge time is extended as less energy is taken in during the early part of the charge and so

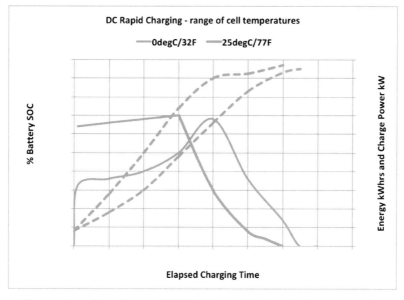

*Illustrative cold and warm DC CCS charges showing the longer time for charging when the battery cells are cold.*

Tests on battery charging at different ambient temperatures also show a variation in charge capacity with a warmer battery capable of taking a higher charge than a cold battery.

AVT-INEL tests showed a difference in battery capacity of about 15% between one battery pack at -6°C/21F compared to one at 35°C/95F.

The charging process itself leads to cell heating; this is true of rapid, fast and, to a lesser extent, slow charging. Hotter cells increase the chemical processes allowing faster charging. If cells get too hot then the charging process can damage the cells themselves and so the BMS will either start the cooling system and/or reduce charge rate until the cells cool.

AVT-INEL has produced considerable amounts of charging information on a number of EVs. On the Nissan Leaf with LMO Pouch Cells, air cooling and battery heating, after a 'normal' drive the following battery pack temperature rises following charging were seen:

- Rapid 50kW DC charger at 2-C the average pack temperature rise at the end of charging was about 6.5°C.

- Level 2 - 7kW/240v charger (~1/3rd C) showed a rise in battery pack temperature of about 2.9°C by the end of each charging session.

These rises are not significant when considered against the change in battery pack temperature changes due to ambient conditions.

This page intentionally blank

## Common Connectors

### AC

SAE J1772 is used in North America and in Japan.

Capable of 80A / 120V-240V AC / <19.2kW.

(Photo Roger Colbeck)

IEC 62196-2 or Mennekes is used in Europe on single and three-phase

Capable of 63A / 230-400V AC / <43kW (max current).

GB/T 20234.2-2011 AC is used in China

Capable of 32A / 220-400V AC / <14kW (max current)

### DC Only

CHAdeMO Yazaki (Nissan, Toyota, and other Japanese manufacturers.)

120A / 500V DC / <60kW (max current).

GB/T 20234.3-2011 DC is used in China

Capable of 250A / 400-750V DC / <187.5kW (max current)

### AC & DC Combo

SAE J1772 DC CCS Combo 1 used in North America and Japan

Capable of 200A / 200-600V DC / <125kW (max current).
(Photo Roger Colbeck)

EU DC CCS Combo 2 used in Europe (BMW, Chysler, Daimler, Ford, General Motors, Volvo, and VW Group.)

Capable of 200A / 200-850V DC / <170kW (max current).

Latest 350kW CCS offers 350A at up to 1000V.

Tesla – proprietary single and three-phase

<250A / <500V DC / <125kW (Dual charger145kW per cabinet)
(Photo Dr Kludge CCA-2)

This page intentionally blank

# Motors, Drives and Transmissions

## Overview

Electric Vehicles (EVs) are powered by electric motors with the energy coming from batteries or generators. EVs can be front drive, rear drive or four wheel drive; distributing electrical power can be done more flexibly electrically than with geared mechanical transmission.

Battery weight, compared to a 'tank' of fossil fuel, has been quite high so it's been important that other systems were as light and compact as possible in order to compensate for this. This situation is changing as batteries get more energy dense and electrical components become more compact, more integrated and lighter in weight so much so that some manufacturers are pursuing adapting a 'standard' ICE vehicle design to battery-electric providing a lower cost solution to the transition from ICE to BEV.

Most motor manufacturers have taken the view that the 'drivetrain, including automotive motors are core technology and specific enough to warrant developing their own motor Intellectual Property.

GM, Hyundai, Kia, and Nissan all use Interior Permanent Magnet Synchronous Machines IPM. BMW use a Hybrid Synchronous Reluctance machine, Jaguar use a Spoke-type PM, and Tesla's 3 uses a Synchronous Reluctance Machine. Renault uses Wound Synchronous, (or Electrically Excited) and Tesla S and X use Induction Machines. Tesla's all-wheel drive Model 3 will use a combination of PM Synchronous Reluctance Machine and Induction Machine.

EV motors in use today are all Alternating Current AC type. Turning the Direct Current DC electricity from the battery into AC suitable for turning the motor is the job of the Inverter. The Inverter takes DC battery power and delivers it to the motor as three-phase AC. For controlling the motor speed, the Inverter uses Pulse Width Modulated Insulated-Gate Bipolar Transistor PWM IGBT: IGBTs were developed over a similar timescale to the Li-Ion battery, and their impact has been as profound as the battery in delivering efficient and usable battery powered vehicles.

Power is transmitted to the wheels (front, rear or all) through a permanently connected, fixed-ratio gear set. In an EV there is no need for a clutch and no need for a multiple gear set: automotive motors can provide instantaneous torque at low speeds and can extend the power through the vehicles speed range without additional gears. Gear changing would simply interrupt energy regeneration and add little useful higher speeds or faster acceleration. Motor maximum rpm for the principal EVs range from 8000 to 15500rm

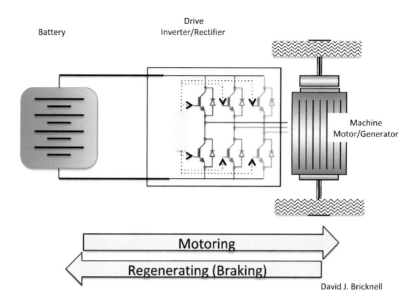

David J. Bricknell

## Types of AC Electric Motors (Machines)

Motor types in use for EVs are all AC and include both Asynchronous (Induction Machines IMs) and Synchronous Machines (Wound Rotor (or Electrically Excited) WRSM or Permanent Magnet PMSM).

The term 'machine' rather than 'motor' would be the more correct one as the machine can either motor or generate - in this book both terms are used.

**Asynchronous 'Induction' Machine** - In an AC Induction Motor IM there is a ring of electromagnets arranged around the outside (stator) and inside that is the rotor that is made up of an axle and coils of wire. The electromagnets in the stator are energized using energy from the battery so that they induce a current in the rotor thereby making the rotor rotate.

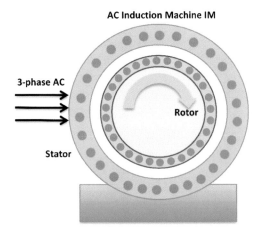

IMs are widely used and are simple, rugged and relatively low cost but are not usually as compact or as efficient as other motors. IMs don't include permanent magnets.

Tesla is the main EV producer using IMs. In the S and X they have adopted a copper rotor cage, rather than the more usual aluminium, in order to improve motor performance but this comes with a higher material cost. For the model 3 Tesla are now using a PMSRM Permanent Magnet Synchronous Reluctance Machine.

**Synchronous Motors** also have a stator providing a ring of electromagnets but instead of inducing a current in the rotor, the rotor is either wound with electromagnets excited by DC current fed from slip rings, or it has a rotor made up from permanent magnets. The synchronous motor rotates at a synchronous speed with speed control implemented by varying the supply frequency. Synchronous machines can be used as either a motor or a generator.

A **Wound Rotor Synchronous Machine** WRSM (also known as an Electrically Excited Synchronous Machine ElExSM) is used by Renault in its Zoe. WSSM are more often associated with very high-power low-speed applications exhibiting high efficiency and a high power factor. WRSMs do not use rare-earth permanent magnets. Renault now uses an in-house designed WRSM in its Zoe having first developed a WRSM motor in collaboration with Continental.

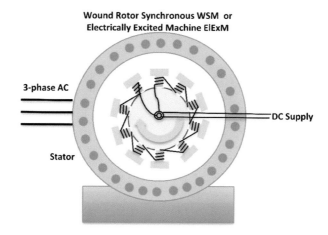

**Permanent Magnet Synchronous Motors PMSM** use permanent magnets to provide the secondary magnetic field in the rotor eliminating the induction heat losses and providing a higher efficiency than an induction motor.

PMSMs are very power dense but can be expensive when rare-earth magnets are used. Some EV manufacturers using PMSMs use rare-earth permanent magnets mounted on the surface SPM and some use them mounted internally IPM. Other motors use ferrite magnets rather than rare earths which can significantly reduce material costs of manufacture.

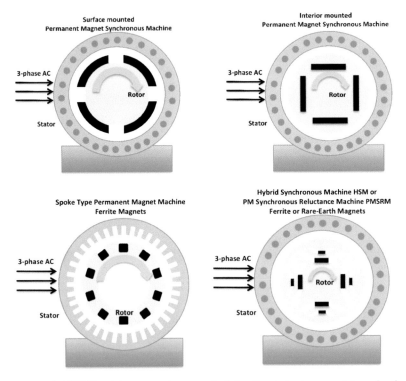

A PMSM with magnets mounted in the interior combines both reluctance torque and magnetic torque to improve efficiency whilst delivering a wide speed range, a high power factor, high efficiency and a very high power density.

This is the **Hybrid Synchronous Motor** used by BMW in its i3 and i8. Ferrous magnets are used in this configuration rather than expensive rare-earth magnets. Tesla use Rare Earth magnets in **Synchronous Reluctance Motor**.

The **Spoke-Type Permanent Magnet Machine** developed by Jaguar achieves high performance and reduced manufacturing costs by the adoption of Ferrite magnets and aluminium windings.

The benefits of the PMSM can be seen in the EPA testing when comparing EPA city cycle and highway cycle for a variety of EVs. All the PMSM vehicle exhibit better City Cycle longer-range performance than their equivalent Highway than IMs; mostly this is attributable to improved low speed motor efficiency

Each motor type exhibits its own efficiency against motor rpm and load.

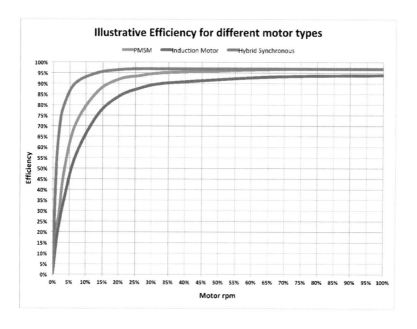

*The above is illustrative of the different motor efficiency throughout the speed range.*

The differences in power available from the different types of motors are captured in the chart below; these show motors from some of the biggest selling EVs and shows the distinctive power curve from each type of machine.

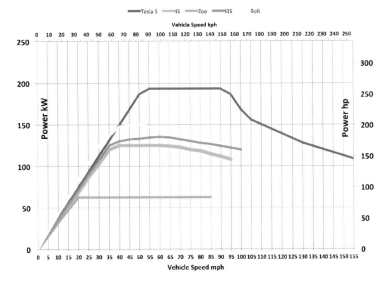

The I-Pace's Spoke-type PMM is expected to have a power curve similar to the i3s HSM. Maximum power is 147kW/197h.p: maximum torque is 348Nm/256lb-ft; maximum rpm is 13,000.

EVs manufacturers use motors in a variety of configurations - for rear wheel drive, for front wheel drive and for all wheel drive sometimes with a single motor rear and twin motors at the front. Reducing the intrusion on the cabin space impacts on motor design – motors drive through a locked-train fixed ratio gear but some drive the shaft through a hollow rotor. GMs Bolt and the new Jaguar I-Pace are using PMSMs with the driveshaft operating through the hollow rotor.

Most electrical motors currently in use in EVs are radial flux (where the flux is radial from the shaft) but considerable interest is being shown axial flux designs (where the flux is along the shaft - think of it as a pancake style motor) because their form factor makes them very suitable for in-wheel hub drive. This technology is being adopted by buses and maybe will in the future also be adopted by trucks. Passenger cars are less likely to do so because of limited wheel diameters but these seem to be increasing in size so maybe this will also happen in the future.

## Power Modules

The Power Module is a Variable Speed Drive that when acting as an **Inverter** controls the electrical motor, converting the DC current from the battery into 3-phase AC and vice versa as a **Rectifier** when the motor acts as a generator.

The power module is part of the electronics responsible for energy management. It takes power from the battery, (and from regeneration, and charging) and distributes power to the motor, to the resistive heating system, the refrigerant compressor, as well as the DC-DC link for powering low voltage vehicle electrical systems and for recharging of the 12V battery.

The DC-DC link reduces the voltage from the HV Battery (~ 360V depending upon battery SOC) to about 14V (similar to an ICE vehicle's alternator output).

The power module usually contains a 3-phase 6-pack configuration of Insulated-Gate Bipolar Transistors IGBTs and emitter-controlled diodes. Tesla uses multiple parallel 6-pack IGBT due to the very high power required.

The power module is one key 'pinch-point' for cooling of the drive train. Power modules are usually direct liquid (water/glycol) cooled through the baseplate with heat being shed through a front mounted radiator.

IGBT modules and Inverter/Rectifiers for EVs are manufactured by companies such as: Infineon, (including International Rectifier), ST Microelectronics, Freescale Semiconductor, NXP Semiconductors, and Texas Instruments.

## Insulated Gate Bipolar Transistor IGBT

Perhaps of not quite the significance to the emergence of competitive Electric Vehicles as the Lithium Ion battery but still an extremely important enabling technology, the Insulated gate Bipolar Transistor is a crucial component contributing to the efficiency of an Electric Vehicle. IGBTs are the key component in the motor drive, the DC-DC link (powering the LV components and recharging the 12V battery), the on-board charger, and the off-board rapid charger.

The IGBT was developed and introduced at a similar time to the Lithium-Ion Battery and was a key milestone in power semiconductor devices. Like LIBS, the latest generation is significantly improved over the first generation

The IGBT is a power semiconductor that has an isolated-gate that allows the very rapid switching on and off of very high currents using just a small voltage applied to the gate: switching frequency is many thousands of times per second. The IGBT can be described as a voltage-controlled bipolar device. Most IGBTs incorporate an anti-parallel or Free Wheeling Diode FWD onto the chip in order to conduct reverse current: the FWD allows regeneration of energy during braking.

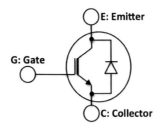

The small 'gate' voltage effectively uses the 1s and 0s of a digital controller and, because of the rapid switching frequency, the IGBT is able to produce a sine-wave from a series of digitally-initiated power pulses; this is called Pulse Width Modulation PWM, and by varying the length of the individual pulses a sine wave (or a wave-form of choice - square wave, stepped wave or a quasi-square wave) can be synthesised as the output. PWM allows smooth and efficient operation free from cogging or torque pulses.

Early motor controls used rheostats for regulating current flow through the motor but were quite inefficient: the energy not being used to drive the motor simply being dumped as heat. Thyristors, developed in the 1950s, are solid-state semiconductors capable of controlling high-power/high-voltage devices and are used extensively in inverters/speed-controllers in megawatt power installations.

Power MOSFETs and IGBTs have replaced Thyristors for lower power applications: Power MOSFETs (Metal Oxide Semiconductor Field Effect Transistor) are used extensively for low-voltage motors and power supplies. The IGBT is a hybrid of the uni-polar MOSFET (which also has an isolated gate) and the Bi-polar Junction Transistor BJT, used extensively in consumer electronics such as amplifiers and radio transmitters.

IGBTs are capable of delivering up to 150kW, switching at 10kHz, and having very low losses at light loads; important for EVs where high motor power is required for acceleration but low power for sustained 'legal' speeds.

As switching frequency increases the waveform will become smoother although because switching losses are proportional to the number of switching events then the higher switching frequencies will incur higher losses that in turn will demand higher cooling.

IGBTs are inherently forward-biased and employ anti-parallel or Free-Wheeling Diode FWD to allow for the reverse inductive current flow seen during regeneration. Regeneration occurs when the motor turns faster than the input current should drive it (known as overhauling); in that condition an inductive current will be passed back into the car and, if not dealt with, could destroy the IGBT. Regenerated power in an EV is recuperated back into the battery.

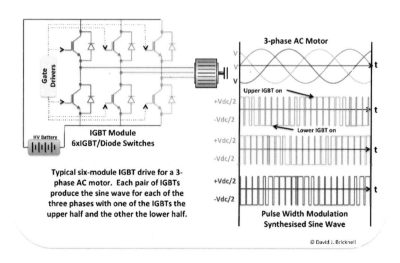

Typical six-module IGBT drive for a 3-phase AC motor. Each pair of IGBTs produce the sine wave for each of the three phases with one of the IGBTs the upper half and the other the lower half.

© David J. Bricknell

Motor drive packs are normally configured with six IGBTs or with multiples of six, i.e. 12, 18 or 24. The power module takes DC at up to 400V and produces 3-phase 360V AC for the Hybrid-Synchronous Motor. Two IGBTs per phase; one IGBT handling the upper half of the sine wave and the other handling the lower half.

There are some efficiency gains to be made from using a multi-layer inverter: instead of 6 IGBTs use 12 or 18 or 36 or more, however costs would increase significantly for a small improvement - the IGBT is a substantial proportion of the inverter cost. Tesla adopts 96 IGBTs in their drive - 16 layers of 6-pack IGBTs are connected in parallel.

For the future, if device costs are reduced, SiC-MOSFETs may replace bipolar IGBT devices in automotive power electronics. SiC-MOSFETs have high efficiency and high power density, exhibit high breakdown voltage, fast switching speeds and low on-resistance, as well as having a higher temperature capability.

Whilst some manufacturers are planning 800V electrical systems, most EVs use a system voltage between 300-400V with the IGBT Power Module rated for 800A/650V. Rating the IGBT at 650V allows some headroom for increasing system voltage during regeneration and other induced voltage peaks. Infineon are also producing 1200V IGBTs suitable for 800V system voltage systems.

The power module inverter/rectifier motor drive is situated close to the electric motor: The power required to be delivered sets one size parameter of the pack but cooling the IGBTs to stay below the maximum junction temperature sets the physical size of the power module. The latest power packs use double sided cooling and have significantly reduced switching losses. High temperatures cause thermal stresses at the junction between the insulating substrate and the chip.

Inverters are most efficient at higher loads but exhibit good efficiency throughout the speed range.

# Drive Train Efficiency

For an ICE vehicle, inefficiencies manifest themselves in combustion, in friction from moving parts and from gear and differential losses through gear meshing. Combustion losses are by far the largest but even gear losses are higher than those incurred in EVs.

For EVs, Drivetrain inefficiencies will include losses from battery, inverter, motor and gear.

Battery

- extracting energy from the battery causes heating of the battery cells and the higher the C-Rate the higher the losses. Similarly the losses will increase with a colder battery cell as extracting energy becomes even less efficient.

Inverter and Motor losses

- converting DC electricity to AC within the Inverter to drive the motors - requiring cooling of the power transistors

- energy losses in the motor from rotor and stator iron and copper losses (eddy currents and hysteresis) and windage and friction losses.

Transmission losses are quite high in an ICE vehicle because of the number of gearwheels in the transmission.
Overall transmission losses will include:
- gear losses from mesh friction including lubrication losses
- bearing losses – rolling/sliding friction and lubrication losses.
- Shaft seals and unions
- Synchronization losses
- clutch fluid drag
- and oil pump

Typical ICE transmissions efficiencies would be
Manual gearbox      92-97%
Automatic Gearbox   90-95%
CVT              87-93%

For EV transmissions most are a simple single-stage spur gear having efficiencies as high as 98-99%.

## Transmissions and Tyres

Electric motors provide full torque at low speeds, unlike an Internal Combustion Engine (ICE), and hence a single-speed transmission can provide the necessary performance across the vehicle operating speed range including quick and smooth acceleration from standing start.

Most drivers' experience is with internal combustion engines, clutches and multi-speed transmission, whether manual or automatic. This leads many to wish for an electric motor coupled to multi-speed transmissions in order to improve efficiency and to reduce the expected noise and vibration that normally accompanies high-revving ICE. There is no need for a clutch as the electric motor doesn't turn until required and when it does it has enough torque not to stall. The motor is a rotary machine and hence inherently has a lower vibration than a reciprocating machine.

ICEs use multi speed transmission so that the engine doesn't stall under the extra loads arising from steep hills, particularly when pulling away – the classic driving test hill-start.

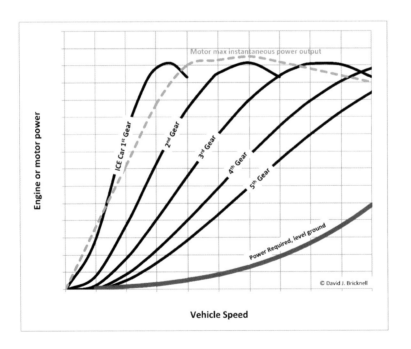

More than one transmission gear means interrupted re-generation, something that plays against energy efficiency

Across the best selling EVs, motor maximum rpm vary from about 7000 to 15500 depending on the motor type. Wheel sizes vary from 16" rim size to 22". Gear reduction ratio depends upon maximum motor rpm and vehicle maximum speed.

Little notice is taken of the performance of tyre size when considering an ICE car. Larger, wider tyres will improve handling performance and grip however there will be a range penalty – Tesla state that on the 85 variants, changing from the 19" to 21" wheel/tyres will reduce range by around 3%. A similar reduction in range (4%) can be seen when changing wheel/tyres on the BMWi3 from 19" to 20". Jaguar's I-Pace, based on WLTP testing show a 12.5% reduction in range between its highest and lowest spec versions with the lowest having 18" and the highest spec having 22".

New tyres will always deliver a shorter range for the first 1000miles/1600km or so while the tyre wears in and a tyre will always produce its best range when it has the least tread depth.

The I-Pace has three options:

- 235/65 R18
- 245/50 R20
- 255/40 R22

Future cars are likely to have larger diameter but narrower and more energy efficient tyres: designers prefer larger diameter wheels and the engineers prefer a narrower tyre for lower rolling resistance. Increasing a tyre diameter by 5cm/2" will lead to a reduction in rolling resistance of about 5% (or 1% per cm / 2.5% per inch), says Michelin's Damien Hallez. Contact patch is similar so grip is maintained.

However increasing wheel size whilst maintaining tyre diameter will increase rolling resistance and will impact negatively on vehicle range.

## I-Pace motors and drives

Two, Spoke-Type, Permanent Magnet Motors each with integral epicyclic gear and final drive, powers the I-Pace. The motors are identical except for the casing that is specific to the front or rear mounting points.

At slower vehicle speeds (~<30mph), the rear motor is used whilst at higher speeds and higher loads/acceleration both motors are used sharing the load equally. Jaguar state that a significant advantage of dual motors is that whilst the rear motor could regenerate up to 60kW, the front motor can manage up to 150kW, offering a potential benefit to range.

The motors produce 147kW drive concentrically through the centre of the rotor thereby keeping the profile very low. The motor maximum rpm is 13,000 and the reduction ratio is 9:1. Dimensions are about 234mm diameter, 500mm long and weight is just 38kg – motor and transmission is just 78kg.

The spoke-type PM motors are to a Jaguar design (a number of patents have been applied for) and are manufactured by American Axle. Spoke type PMs have a high torque density but require careful design manage the back electromotive force EMF inherent in the design.

*The front of two concentric spoke-type Permanent Magnet Motors looking aft and showing the motor and inverter stack.*
*(Photo Halit Murat Gültekin)*

The advantage for Jaguar in using this type of motor is the ability to use Ferrite magnets, rather than Rare-Earth magnets enabling a significant reduction in material costs. Jaguar has further reduced costs by adopting aluminium windings in place of copper.

The Inverters, also Jaguar's design, are capable of up to 550A and are close-coupled to the motors although maybe not quite as close as the latest from other EV manufacturers – Jaguar intends in the future to make the inverters part of the motor as Tesla and BMW have done recently.

*View looking forward towards the motor and inverter stack.*
*(Photo Halit Murat Gültekin*

*View looking aft towards the rear motor and inverter stack.*
*(Photo Halit Murat Gültekin*

This page intentionally blank

# COOLING AND HEATING

David J Bricknell

This page intentionally blank

## Overview

Cooling and/or heating normally isn't something that would feature much when discussing ICE cars but it can have a considerable impact on vehicle range. For vehicles such as the i-Pace the proportionate impact remains similar but the occasions when it becomes a concern is only for very long journeys.

EVs use a number of different technologies for cooling of key components including active and passive air, water-glycol and refrigerants. Cooling of an EV's motor, drive electronics, and battery is critical to the Electric Vehicle's continuous performance.

Cabin cooling uses the same refrigerant technology as an ICE car but heating, because of the lack of engine waste heat, uses either electric resistive coils or electrically driven reverse refrigerant-cycle heat pumps. Heat pumps can be around three times more efficient for cabin heating than resistive heating.

Waste heat from cooling drives, motors and batteries isn't currently used directly for cabin heating because of the relatively low temperatures but used in conjunction with a heat pump and efficiency is much improved.

For the I-Pace, heating of the cabin interior is energy efficient due to the adoption of a heat pump - approximately 1kW of power is used to deliver 2.5kW of heat at its optimum efficiency. Jaguar have adopted best practice by scavenging waste heat from the electrical and electronics systems meaning that once underway, with the motors warm, the heat pump efficiency stays high even at very low ambient temperatures.

The heat pump used in reverse cycle is also used for battery heating whereas most EVs will use the less efficient resistive heating.

# Range impact

At low vehicle speeds, in very cold temperatures, the maximum energy demand for an electrical vehicle can come from the heating and ventilation system.

For an ICE car it's been normal, since around the 1960s, to have a cabin heating system using waste heat from the internal combustion process; car-sized internal combustion engines have a rather poor efficiency with a significant amount of waste heat which is either rejected through the car's radiator or redirected to cabin heating, essentially for 'free'. This amount of 'free' waste heat isn't available to the more efficient electric car.

Since the 2000s, in many countries, Air Conditioning A/C has become increasingly a 'standard specification'. There is a noticeable increase in an ICE car's fuel consumption and decrease in its range (~8%-10%) when running A/C.

For an EV, range will be impacted whenever a cooling A/C demand is made. However what comes as a surprise to many first time EV drivers with 20-30kWhr battery packs is the magnitude of that impact on range when heating the car interior during very cold ambient outside temperatures.

The graph opposite shows a typical reduction in range arising from the use of battery-stored energy to heat the car interior. A typical UK Summer's day will draw neither heat nor cooling but either side of that an impact is seen on range.

New EV drivers' often say 'there's something wrong with my battery' once winter comes but the impact is more likely coming from cabin heating. Evidence of the magnitude of the demand is supported by 'fleetcarma's' analysis of a number of EVs and an analysis by the Institute for Powertrains and Automotive Technology.

Direct sunlight will cause a significant shift in the peak range by maybe five or 10°C lower in ambient temperature; such is the thermal gain from solar energy in modern vehicles glassy cockpits. In sunny climates window tinting may be beneficial; in cooler climates keep them clear.

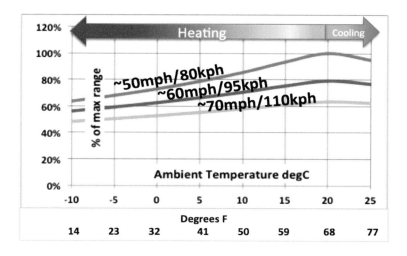

*Typical range adjustment allowing for both vehicle speed and for cabin cooling and heating for Electric Vehicles.*

*Cabin heating varies with time and propulsion power varies with speed so the slower you go the greater the impact of cabin heating will be*

## Heating and Cooling

EVs have a number of heating and cooling systems. Given the relative simplicity of a battery and electric motor, the heating and cooling system is quite complex - EVs need to heat and/or cool the battery and the car's interior. It also needs to cool the motor and its motor drive inverter/rectifier, and the battery charging rectifiers.

Waste heat from motors, inverters or batteries is today not directly used to heat cabins however Jaguar, with its I-Pace, does use the waste heat from motor inverter cooling to improve the efficiency of its heat pump at low ambient temperatures as well as using this low level waste heat for battery warming.

Battery cooling varies across EVs – battery life will be reduced when stored or operated at high temperatures and will also be reduced when the EV is being driven hard or rapidly charged when the battery is very cold.

Some EVs adopt passive cooling for battery temperature management some use active air cooling, some use a water glycol mix, and some use refrigerants. Battery heating, where incorporated, is usually by resistive heating although the latest Tesla's use parasitic heating from zero-speed motor load. The I-Pace uses water-glycol at lower temperatures but couples this system with the refrigerant cooling to combat higher temperature rises.

## Cabin Heating

For cabin heating a circulating water-glycol system is used with heat provided to the system either by a number of electrical heating coils or by a heat pump. Heat is transferred to the cabin by a heat exchanger and fan system.

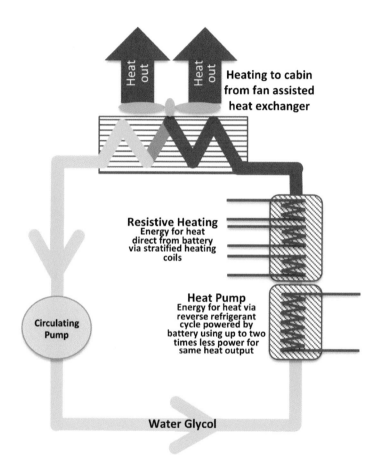

## Heat Pumps and Refrigerant Cycle

Heat pumps, using the refrigerant cycle to deliver either cabin heat (or cabin cooling), can, dependent on how low ambient temperature is, be significantly more efficient than resistive heating and its additional cost, weight and complexity can be justified when ensuring as much range as possible is maintained in winter months.

Think of the Heat Pump as a refrigerator inside out - the grille on the back of the fridge is the condenser and gets hot as the refrigerant gas becomes a liquid whereas the inside of the fridge get cold as the refrigerant turns from a liquid to a gas. The vehicle cabin is the outside of the fridge and the inside of the fridge is now the atmosphere.

The refrigerant cycle produces heat (or cold) on about a ratio of one unit of energy to two units of heat or three units of cold by using the energy liberated when changing from liquid to gas or gained from changing the gas to liquid and is hence a very efficient means of heating and or cooling.   Whether heat or cold is desired is purely down to direction of the cycle and hence the positioning of the evaporator and the condenser.

Battery energy is used to drive the compressor but ambient heat is used to evaporate the refrigerant.  As the ambient temperature drops closer to the boiling point of the refrigerant, the efficiency of the system drops markedly as the amount of heat easily extracted from the atmosphere will fall.  Jaguar, and a number of other manufacturers now use the waste heat from the motor and electronics to provide a higher effective ambient temperature thereby maintaining efficiency to quite low temperatures.

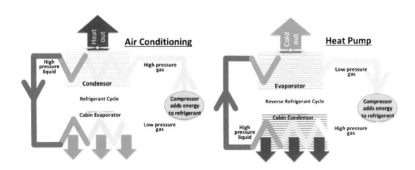

*The above diagram showing the refrigerant cycle can operate in two ways – when hot, the condenser ejects heat to outside the car and delivers cold air into the car whereas when cold, the condenser is repurposed as an evaporator and ejects cold air top the outside whilst delivering hot air from the condenser into the car.*

The refrigerant cycle can be two to three times more efficient than a resistive heating coil depending upon external ambient temperature or, in the case of the I-Pace, the temperature of the electrical cooling system.

Using refrigerants is efficient because heat is extracted when turning the refrigerant liquid into a gas and in reverse the refrigerant gives up heat when condensing from a gas to a liquid.

The refrigerants used most often for EVs are R-1234yf or R-134a. The normal boiling point of R1234yf is minus 29°C/-20F (R134a is minus 26°C/-15F) and, when turning the liquid refrigerant into a gas, heat will be extracted from the cabin or the battery. R-1234yf has a Global Warming Potential GWP of just 4, whereas R134a (a HFC) has a GWP of 1440 and R-12 (a CFC, that is now no longer used) had a GWP of 8500. Jaguar uses R1234yf. Some manufacturers (Mercedes and VAG) are adopting $CO_2$ (R-744) with a GWP of 1 but this comes with much higher pressures and a number of other engineering challenges.

When used as a heat pump the heat comes from the atmosphere with the condenser being re-assigned as an evaporator. This is the same way that an air-source heat-pump uses atmospheric heat for a home installation. As the ambient temperature gets colder, the I-Pace will use the electrics waste heat to improve efficiency.

In an EV a 2:1 ratio for heating and a 3:1 for cooling is a guide

The refrigerant system uses a:

- compressor, to add energy to the refrigerant making it a higher pressure gas at a hotter temperature

- condenser, to turn the higher pressure gas to a high pressure liquid thereby releasing heat

- evaporator to 'boil' the liquid to a gas thereby extracting heat from the cabin (and battery, if refrigerant is also used for battery cooling).

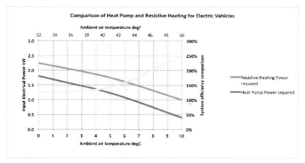

## Drivetrain cooling

Whilst the EV motor and its drive electronics (inverter/rectifier) are very efficient they are also very power-dense: waste heat removal is a key area if performance is not to be reduced.

Similarly, the charging electronics with its integral AC/DC rectifier requires cooling whilst in use.

These three components use a common water-glycol cooling circuit disposing of heat through a conventional front-mounted radiator with integral electric fan – a surprise to many EV drivers is that their car has a radiator and radiator fan.

*An EV showing the front mounted cooling radiator.*
*Photo courtesy of Rory Fitzgerald.*

Both motor and drives for the I-Pace are highly efficient across a broad operating range. The electric machine mostly operating between 90-95% efficiency but at lower speeds and higher acceleration loads the efficiency can drop. Similarly whilst the IGBT-based inverter will see high efficiencies at high motor rpms (high vehicle speeds), at lower motor rpm efficiencies will drop off.

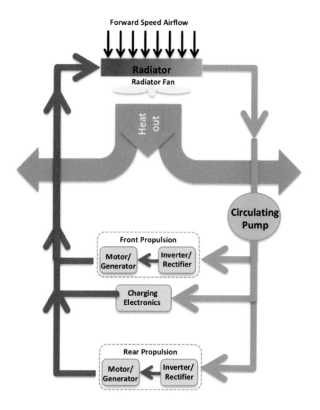

Coolant temperatures can reach up to around 85°C/185F but unlike an Internal Combustion Engine this isn't an operating temperature to be reached in order to maximize efficiency but is something that will vary throughout the vehicle's use.

If the electronics waste heat is also used for battery warming then a thermostat can be included on this circuit.

The I-Pace configures the cooling and heating system to control temperatures in three key components or areas – battery, motors/drives, and the cabin.

A circulating water-glycol system coupled to a radiator is used to cool the motors and drives and also to cool the charging electronics when in use. Jaguar, however, also use this waste-heat to warm the battery to its optimum operating temperature and also to improve the efficiency of the heat pump when ambient temperatures are very low.

A refrigerant cycle is used for Air Conditioning and is used in reverse cycle for the heat pump. Both cycles are also used through a heat exchanger to either warm or chill the battery coolant.

The complexity of the system is justified by the improvement in range and the longer lifecycle of the battery cells. Not all EV manufacturers adopt such a level of complexity.

The following four diagrams are intended to illustrate the operation of the system at various ambient temperatures. The number of combinations of heating and cooling can be quite large given that battery and power electronics temperatures are as much a function of driving style and journey type as it is ambient air temperature and cabin temperature is very much a personal choice.

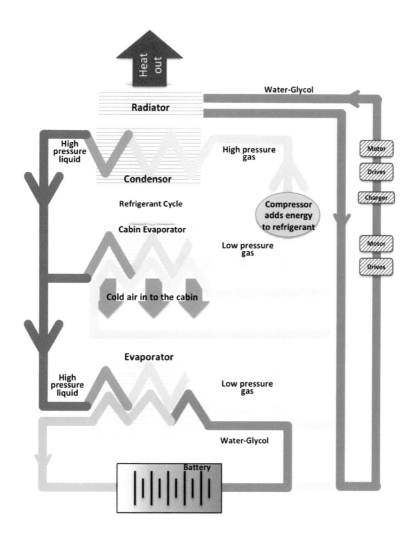

*Very Hot Conditions*

*Cabin cooled with refrigerant*

*Battery cooled with refrigerant*

*Power electronics and motor cooled with water-glycol system and radiator*

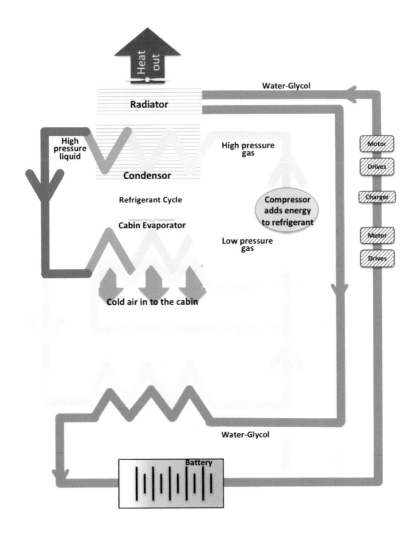

*Hot Conditions*

*Cabin cooled with refrigerant*

*Battery, Power electronics and motor cooled with water-glycol system and radiator*

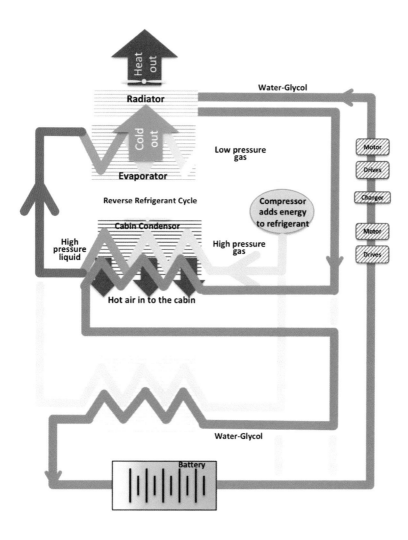

*Cold Conditions*

*Cabin heated with heat pump and waste Heat from power electronics and motor.*

*Battery warmed by water-glycol system taking heat from power electronics and motor*

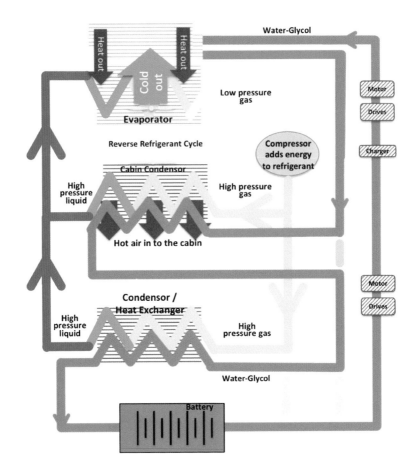

### Very Cold Conditions

*Cabin and Battery warmed by Heat Pump*

*Motor and Electronics waste heat used in evaporator to improve low temperature refrigeration cycle*

# Bibliography

- Advanced power electronics and electric motors - vehicle technologies office, 2012, US Department of Energy
- Advanced Vehicle Testing Activity - Idaho National Laboratory
- Alternative motor technologies for traction drives of hybrid and electric vehicles - Dr Sab Safi CEng, SDT Drive Technology
- A guide to Electric Vehicle Infrastructure - BEAMA
- Battery cell balancing: what to balance and how - Yevgen Barsukov, Texas Instruments
- Battery Electric Vehicles in practice - cost, range, environment, convenience - Austrian Society of Automotive Engineers
- Battery pack design for commercial EV propulsion - Sean Lamprell, MIRA
- Benchmarking EV and HEV technologies - Tim Burress, Oak Ridge National Laboratory
- BMW & Solid Power to jointly develop solid-state batteries for electric vehicles
- CARB 2012 Amendments to the Zero Emission Vehicle Regulations
- Cell balancing buys extra run time and battery life - Sihua Wen
- Combined Charging System 1.0 Specification
- Design of the Chevrolet Bolt EV Propulsion System – Liu, J., Anwar, M., Chiang, P., Hawkins, S. et al., SAE Int. J. Alt. Power 5(1): 79-86 2016  https://doi.org/10.4271/2016-01-1153.
- Detailed Loss Modelling of Vehicle Gearboxes – Schlegel, Hosl, and Diel.
- Development of an Electric Motor for a Newly Developed Electric Vehicle  - Tohru Nakada, Shigeaki Ishikawa, and Shunji Oki
- Development of Automotive Air-Conditioning Systems by Heat Pump Technology - Kondo, Katayama, Suetake and Morishita
- "Downloadable Dynamometer Database (http://www.transportation.anl.gov/D3/) Advanced Powertrain Research Facility (APRF) at Argonne National Laboratory under the funding and guidance of the U.S. Department of Energy (DOE)"
- Effects of Electric Vehicle fast charging on battery life and vehicle performance - Matthew Shirk and Jeffrey Wishart
- Electric Vehicle Battery Technologies - Kwo Young, Caisheng Wang, Le Yi Wang and Kai Strunz

- Electric vehicle traction motors without rare earth magnets - James D. Widmer, Richard Mann, Mohammed Kimiabeigi

- Enabling Fast Charging – A Technology Gap Assessment – US Dept of Energy

- Our guide to batteries – Johnson Matthey Battery Systems

- Has Samsung SDI cracked the graphene puzzle – clean technica

- High performance low cost electric motor for electric vehicles using ferrite magnets – Kimiabeigi, Widmer, Long, Gao, Goss, Martin, Lisle, Vizan, Michaelides and Mecrow

- Johnson Matthey To Put £200 Million Into Batteries In 2018 | CleanTechnica

- Infineon Company Presentation September 12, 2013
  Infineon HybridPack 2 - general information

- Interfacial challenges in solid-state Li-Ion batteries  Seung-Tack Myung, Filippo Maglia, Kang-Joon Park, Chong Seung Yoon, Peter Lamp, Sung-Jin Kim and Yang-Kook Sun

- Introduction to Batteries  - Martin Green – Director Battery Technologies.

- Li-Ion battery materials present and future – Naoki Nitta, Feixiang Wu, Jung Tae Lee, and Gleb Yushin

- nickel-iron-battery.com

- Plug in Electric Vehicle and Infrastructure Analysis - September 2015 Idaho National Laboratory

- Report-on-the-needs-for-interoperability-between-EVs-and-electrical-power-system
  COTEVOS_D1.1_needs_for_interoperability _v1.0 66-358 EU Project no. 608934

- Regenerative braking in an electric vehicle - Jarrad Cody, Özdemir Göl, Zorica Nedic, Andrew Nafalski, Aaron Mohtar University of South Australia

- SAE International standards work, including communication protocols and connectors, fast charge, batteries - Jack Pokrzywa, Director SAE Ground Vehicle Standards

- IA-HEV Task 20 "Quick Charging Technology" - Ignacio Martín Jiménez Carlos Arsuaga Carreras Gregorio Fernández Aznar José Francisco Sanz Osorio - CIRCE (Spain)

- Smart equipment and systems for electric vehicle charging - Technology for energy efficiency

- Steady State Vehicle Charging fact Sheet - Advanced Vehicle Testing Activity - Idaho National Laboratory
- Tesla tweaks its battery chemistry: a closer look at silicon anode development Posted September 23, 2015 by Christian Ruoff ChargeDevs
- The Tesla Roadster battery system, Tesla Motors – August 2016 Gene Berdichevsky, Kurt Kelty, JB Straubel, and Erik Toomre,
- Theory of SEI Formation in rechargeable batteries: capacity fade, accelerated ageing and lifetime prediction – Matthew B. Pinson and Martin Z. Bezant
- The Battery University
- The energy requirement of battery electric vehicles under different conditions - Institute for Powertrains and Automotive Technology - Dr. Werner Tober
- The hybrid-synchronous machine of the new BMW i3 & i8 - Dr. Ing J. Merweth, BMW Group, Munich
- The Tesla battery Report - Manahem Anderman - Advanced Automotive batteries
- The high voltage batteries of the BMWi3 and BMWi8  - Dipl.-Ing. Florian Schoewel, Dipl-Ing. Elmar Hockgeiger BMW Group, München
- Understanding Lithium-Ion Technology - Jim McDowall, Saft America, Inc.
- Will your battery survive a world with fast chargers - Jeremy S. Neubauer and Eric Wood, National Renewable Energy Laboratory

# Glossary

**Battery** – a device that delivers electrical energy from chemical energy.

**Battery Cell** – the building block of a battery pack. Each cell contains an anode, a cathode, a separator and an electrolyte. For Li-Ion, each cell will produce a nominal 3.6 – 3.8V. Battery Cells can be 'primary' (not rechargeable) or 'secondary' (rechargeable). All EV batteries are secondary.

**Battery Module** – is a collection of battery cells and is the smallest Line Replaceable Unit LRU of the battery pack.

**Battery Pack** – is a collection of modules with a single thermal management system. Some EVs may have more than one pack.

**Capacity** – Ampere-Hour (Ah) is the nominal capacity at a specified temperature and discharge rate. For the i3 this is 60Ah and with the latest battery, 94Ah.

**Capacity,** rated –Watt hours or kiloWatt hours is the Ampere-Hours times the nominal voltage time the number of cells.

**Current, Maximum Discharge** – is the maximum current that can be delivered by the battery without sustaining damage. For the 60Ah BMW i3 this is ~ 110A. Along with the max continuous motor power this limits the car's continuous maximum speed.

**Current, Max 30-sec discharge pulse current** - is the maximum current that can be delivered in a 30-second pulse. For the BMW i3 this is ~ 400A and along with the motor peak power (and gearing) determines the car's maximum acceleration.

**Current, recommended charge current** – is the current that the vessel charges at before reaching the constant voltage phase. For the 60Ah i3 this is 110 Amps.

**Battery Reversal** – if a series connected set of battery cells isn't regularly balanced the weakest cell will continue to get weaker at every charge and discharge until at some point the cell will reverse its voltage causing a complete failure, often catastrophic, of the battery pack.

**Battery Management System BMS** – is the system, software and hardware that monitors and controls the charging and discharging of the battery and the battery temperature.

**Calendar Life** – is the life span of the battery under storage. It will be affected by temperature and SOC. Together with cycle-life this determines overall battery life.

**C-Rate** – is the battery capacity charged or discharged in one-hour.

**Cathode** - During Charging the ions move from Cathode to Anode. During discharge ions move from Anode to Cathode. The Cathode material is

122

either a lithium mixed-metal oxide (typically NMC, NCA or LMO), lithium iron phosphate, or, in the case of LTO, graphite.

**Cycle Life** – is the number of charge and discharge cycles at a specified Depth of Discharge DOD (normally 80% of absolute SOC) that the battery can undergo before failing to meet its manufacturer's defined end-of-life. The i3 is expected to undergo 1000 complete cycles before its SOH falls below 70%. BMW warrants the i3 battery for 8-years or 100,000 miles whichever is earliest. Cycle Life is affected by temperature and C-Rate. Together with Calendar Life this determines overall battery life.

**Calendar Life** – is the life span of the battery under storage. It will be affected by temperature and SOC. Together with cycle-life this determines overall battery life.

**Depth of Discharge DOD** – is the amount (%) of battery discharged compared to the maximum capacity of the battery. The higher the DOD, the lower the battery life.

**Electrolyte** – the electrolyte allows the ions to move from anode to cathode and back again. It is normally a liquid or gel of lithium salts and solvents. Considerable interest exists in a solid electrolyte.

**Internal Resistance** – varies with charging and discharging as well as under different operating conditions, such as C-Rate and temperature – hence it affects battery capacity and battery power. Increasing Internal resistance means reducing battery efficiency leading to greater battery temperature.

**Lithium-Polymer** – uses a microporous polymer in place of the separator. The polymer is covered by an electrolytic gel that acts as a catalyst that improves the efficiency of the chemical reaction.

**Power Density** – is the battery peak power (kW) per battery pack unit volume (litres). For the i3 this is 147kW and a battery pack volume of 191 litres ~ 0.77kW/l

**State of Charge SOC** – is an estimate of the amount of usable energy remaining in the battery. Given that this will vary with rate of charge or discharge and cell temperature this is a difficult criteria to quantify accurately.

**State of Health SOH** – is a measure of the battery charge capacity compared to the charge capacity when the battery was new.

**Specific Energy** – is a measure of the capacity of the battery (Watt hours) per battery mass (kg). The i3 battery pack is 21.6/18.8kWhrs in 236kg ~ 92/80kWhr/kg.

**Specific Power** – is a measure of the battery peak power (kW) per battery pack mass (kg). For the i3 this is 147kW in 236kg ~ 0.62kW/kg.

**Voltage, Cut-off** – is the cell voltage at 'empty' as determined by the supplier and monitored by the Battery Management System.

**Voltage, Terminal** – is the voltage the battery delivers under load and will reduce with reducing battery SOC.

**Voltage, Nominal** – is taken as the average voltage of the battery cell and is between the maximum and minimum voltage.

**Voltage, Open Circuit** – is the no-load cell voltage

**Voltage, Charge** – is the voltage that the cell is charged at. For a Li-Ion this increases during the constant-current charge phase, typically up to about 70%, and is steady at the constant-voltage phase allowing the charge current to gradually reduce until the battery is fully charged.

# About the Author

David J. Bricknell began his engineering career as an apprentice in Her Majesty's Royal Dockyard in Devonport and subsequently he studied Ship Science and Engineering at the University of Southampton.

His career in the marine world involved ship repair, ship-building, electronics and engineering at a number of large UK engineering companies (Vosper Thornycroft and British Aerospace) as well as consultancy at leading UK-based global engineering company, British Maritime Technology.

At Rolls-Royce Ltd, David led the Naval design, power and propulsion sector, publishing over thirty technical papers around the world: the principles and technologies of power and propulsion being broadly similar across ships and vehicles

A responsibility for R&D as well as marine-wide business development provided the breadth of understanding across engines, transmissions as well as electrical machines, drives and energy storage.

David continues his engineering career through his own consultancy, Brycheins Ltd.

44645456R00081

Printed in Poland
by Amazon Fulfillment
Poland Sp. z o.o., Wrocław